NEW LEFT REVIEW 143

SECOND SERIES

SEPTEMBER OCTOBER 2023

PROGRAMME NOTES

PERRY ANDERSON: The Standard of Civilization

A world order governed by the rule of law is the mainstay of the West's claim to leadership. A host of institutions, topped by the UN itself, lend this principle material form. But what is the juridical nature of international law? History, theory and practice of a powerful hegemonic instrument.

CAITLÍN DOHERTY: Topographies of Capital

Engagement with the recent work of leading American socialist feminist Nancy Fraser, drawing out continuities between *Cannibal Capitalism*'s multi-dimensional account of the present conjuncture—encompassing crises of capitalist accumulation, gendered social reproduction, global warming and democratic politics—and Fraser's earlier theses on recognition, redistribution and representation.

ALYSSA BATTISTONI & GEOFF MAN: Climate Bidenomics

What light do the contradictions of Democratic climate policy throw on the situation of American capitalism today? In reply to Riley and Brenner's 'Seven Theses' (NLR 138), positing a post-growth regime of accumulation with bitterly divided zero-sum politics, Battistoni and Mann see a flawed attempt at a green-growth strategy, its lopsided logic exemplified in the current autoworkers' strike.

CONTRIBUTORS

ALYSSA BATTISTONI: *teaches political theory at Barnard; co-author of* A Planet to Win *(2019); see also* NLR *135 and* Sidecar

JOHANNES HOERNING: *studies political philosophy at Cambridge; see also* Sidecar

NIC JOHNSON: *studies history at the University of Chicago*

GEOFF MANN: *teaches geography at Simon Fraser University; author of* In the Long Run We Are All Dead *(2017) and co-author of* Climate Leviathan *(2018); see also* NLR *56*

CHRISTOPH SCHURINGA: *teaches philosophy at Northeastern University London; editor of the* Hegel Bulletin.

PERRY ANDERSON

THE STANDARD

OF CIVILIZATION

I N 1929 LUCIEN FEBVRE offered the first systematic reflection
on the evolution of the meanings of the term 'civilization', from
singular ideal, which he dated to the third quarter of the 18th century, to plural fact, which he placed at the close of the Napoleonic
epoch. In 1944–45 he devoted his last lecture course to 'Europe: genesis
of a civilization', and a year later added the word *Civilisations* to *Économies
et Sociétés* in the title of the *Annales* journal itself. Just before he died,
he penned a sharp note approving a colleague's dismissal of Valéry's
famous dictum that this civilization had now realized it was mortal:
'In fact, it is not civilizations that are mortal. The current of civilization
persists across passing eclipses . . . Sober deflation of a windbag.'[1] A decade later, Fernand Braudel would concur: 'When Paul Valéry declared
"Civilizations, we know you to be mortal", he was surely exaggerating.
The seasons of history cause the flowers and the fruit to fall, but the tree
remains. At the very least, it is much harder to kill.'[2]

How far has Braudel's confidence—that usage of the term in the singular was no longer of much significance—proved justified? One way
of approaching this is to look at a body of thought and practice where
'civilization' was historically conspicuous, namely international law.
There, we can start by noting what might appear a paradox. The contemporary notion of international law immediately evokes the idea of
relations between sovereign states. In the West, these relations are generally held to have developed into something like a formal system for the
first time with the Treaty of Westphalia, which in 1648 brought an end
to the Thirty Years' War in Europe. It would seem logical to assume that
a developed body of thought about international law would have arisen

around this turning-point. In fact, however, to pinpoint its origins we must go back to the 1530s. It was then that its history really started, in the writing of the Spanish theologian Francisco de Vitoria, whose concern was not with relations between the states of Europe, of which Spain was at that time much the most powerful, but with relations between Europeans—preeminently, of course, Spaniards—and the peoples of the newly discovered Americas.

Foundations

Drawing on Roman notions of a *ius gentium*, or law of nations, Vitoria asked by what right Spain had recently come into possession of the larger part of the Western hemisphere. Was it because these lands were uninhabited, or because the Pope had allocated them to Spain, or because it was a duty to convert pagans to Christianity, if necessary by force? Vitoria rejected all such grounds for conquest of the New World. Did that mean it was therefore contrary to the law of nations? It did not, because when the Spaniards arrived in their lands, the savage inhabitants of the Americas had violated the universal 'right of communication'— *ius communicandi*—that was an essential principle of the law of nations. What did such 'communication' mean? It meant freedom to travel and freedom to buy and sell, anywhere: in other words, freedom of trade and freedom to persuade, that is, to preach Christian truths to the Indians, as Spaniards called them. If Indians resisted these rights, the Spaniards were justified in defending themselves by force, building fortresses, seizing land and waging war against them in retribution. Should the Indians persist in their misdeeds, they were to be treated as treacherous foes, subject to plunder and enslavement.[3] The Conquests were therefore, after all, perfectly legitimate.

The first real building-block of what would, for another two hundred years, still be called the law of nations was thus constructed as a justification of Spanish imperialism. The second, still more influential, building-block came with the writing of Hugo Grotius in the early 17th century. Grotius is mainly remembered, and admired, today for his

---

[1] Lucien Febvre, 'Une Histoire de la civilisation', *Annales*, October–December 1950, p. 492, reviewing Joseph Chappey's *Histoire générale de la civilisation d'Occident de 1870 à 1950*.
[2] Fernand Braudel, *Grammaire des civilisations*, Paris 1963.
[3] Francisco de Vitoria, *Relecciones sobre los Indios* [1538/9], Madrid 1946, I, 3: 1, 2, 6, 7, 8.

treatise on 'The Law of War and Peace'—*De iure belli ac pacis*—of 1625. But his actual entry into international law, as we now understand it, began with a text that would come to be known as 'On Booty'—*De iure praedae*—written twenty years earlier. In this document, Grotius set out a legal justification for the seizure by a captain of the Dutch East India Company, one of his cousins, of a Portuguese ship carrying copper, silk, porcelain and silver to the value of three million guilder, a figure comparable to the total annual revenue of England at the time—an act of plunder on an unprecedented scale, causing a sensation in Europe. In its fifteenth chapter, subsequently published as *Mare Liberum*, Grotius explained that the high seas should be regarded as a free zone for both states and armed private companies, and his cousin was well within his rights—so providing a legal brief for Dutch commercial imperialism, as Vitoria had for Spanish territorial imperialism.

By the time Grotius came to write his general treatise on the laws of war and peace, two decades later, the Dutch had become interested in colonies on land too, soon seizing parts of Brazil from Portugal, and Grotius now argued that Europeans had the right to wage war on any peoples, even if they were not attacked by them, whose customs they regarded as barbarous, as retribution for their crimes against nature. This was *ius gladii*—the right of the sword, or of punishment. He wrote: 'Kings, and those who are invested with a power equal to kings, have a right to exact punishments not only for injuries committed against themselves, or their Subjects, but likewise, for those which do not peculiarly concern them, but are, in any persons whatsoever, grievous violations of the Law of Nature or Nations.'[4] In other words, Grotius offered licence to attack, conquer and kill whosoever stood in the way of European expansion.

To these two cornerstones of early modern international law, *ius communicandi* and *ius gladii*, were added two more justifications for colonization of the world beyond Europe. Thomas Hobbes proposed an argument from demography: there were too many people at home, and so few people overseas that European settlers in hunter-gatherer lands had the right, not to 'exterminate those they find there; but constrain them to inhabit closer together, and not range a great deal of ground, to snatch what they find'[5]—a straightforward programme for the reservations into which the native inhabitants of North America would eventually

---

4 Hugo Grotius, *De Jure Belli ac Pacis*, II, XL.
5 Thomas Hobbes, *Leviathan*, Oxford 2012, p. 540.

be driven. Obviously, if lands could simply be deemed unoccupied, even this would be unnecessary. To that widely held view, John Locke added the further argument that if there were local inhabitants on the spot, but they failed to make the *best use* of the land available to them, then Europeans had every legal right to deprive them of it, since they would fulfill God's purpose for it by increasing the productivity of the soil.[6] With this, the repertoire of justifications for European imperial expansion was, by the end of the 17th century, complete; the rights of communication, of punishment, of occupation and of production all warranted seizure of the rest of the planet.

Limited to the civilized

By the 18th century, relations between states within Europe had become the foreground of writings on the law of nations, and there were voices of the Enlightenment—Diderot, Smith, Kant among them—questioning the morality of colonial seizures of lands beyond Europe, though none actually proposed reversing them. Characteristically, far the most influential of the new treatises, *Le Droit des gens*, was by the Swiss thinker Emer de Vattel. In it, Vattel coolly remarked: 'The earth belongs to all mankind and was designed to furnish them with subsistence: if each nation had from the beginning resolved to appropriate to itself a vast country, that the people might live only by hunting, fishing and wild fruits, our globe would not be sufficient to maintain a tenth part of its present inhabitants. We do not therefore deviate from the views of nature in confining the Indians within narrower limits.'[7]

Continuous in this respect with its predecessors, Vattel's work nevertheless marked a discursive turning-point, towards a more secular version of the divinely decreed laws of nature justifying earlier versions of the law of nations. Without in any way disappearing, religion ceased to be the first-order warrant for the colonization of the rest of the world. That position passed, henceforward, to another term. Vattel's treatise was published in 1758. Just one year earlier, in 1757, appeared the first traceable use of the noun *civilization*—still absent from the relevant volume of *Encyclopédie*

---

[6] John Locke, *Two Treatises of Government* II, § 32–46.

[7] As for nomads: 'Those peoples (such as the ancient Germans, and some modern Tartars), who inhabit fertile countries, but disdain to cultivate their lands, and chuse rather to live by plunder, are wanting to themselves, are injurious to all their neighbours, and deserve to be extirpated as savage and pernicious beasts': VII, § 81. Emer de Vattel, *Le Droit des gens, ou Principes de la loi naturelle*, XVIII, § 209.

that had come out in 1753—in a text by Mirabeau's father. Within a few years, Adam Ferguson introduced it, independently, in Scotland.

The success of Vattel's work, principally concerned with relations between European states, but covering their relations with the rest of the world, was inseparable from its timing. It appeared in the midst of the first global conflict, the Seven Years' War pitting France against Britain, fought out not only in Europe, but in North America, the Caribbean, the Indian Ocean and South-East Asia—in its turn, a dress-rehearsal for the titanic struggles within Europe, with their extensions across the world, unleashed by the French Revolution. By the time these came to an end with the victory of the combined *anciens régimes* over Napoleon in 1815, three significant changes to what had once been the law of nations had occurred. In 1789, criticizing the ambiguity of the formula—wasn't *jus gentium* a misnomer for *jus inter gentes?*—Bentham coined the term 'international law', which gradually took hold in the next century. By then, the normative dividing line between Europe and the rest of the world had become 'civilization', rather than primarily the Christian religion, although the latter remained a vital attribute of the former.

Lastly, in the second decade of the 19th century, where Vattel had in keeping with the diplomatic conventions of the time assumed the nominal equality of sovereign states, the Congress of Vienna for the first time introduced a formal hierarchy of states *within* Europe, a distinction of rank between five 'Great Powers'—the so-called Pentarchy of England, Russia, Austria, Prussia and France—which were accorded special privileges and settled the map of the continent, and every other state. This was an innovation designed to seal the unity of the counter-revolutionary coalition that had defeated Napoleon and restored monarchies throughout Europe. But it was one which outlasted the Restoration period itself. By the 1880s, the leading Scottish jurist James Lorimer could remark that the equality of states 'may now, I think, safely be said to have been repudiated by history', not to speak of reason, as a 'more transparent fiction than the equality of all individuals'.[8]

Together with these changes came the emergence, alongside classical diplomacy, of international law as a profession. Its first major statement came from a former American ambassador to Prussia, Henry Wheaton,

---

[8] James Lorimer, *The Institutes of the Law of Nations: A Treatise of the Jural Relations of Separate Political Communities*, Edinburgh and London 1883, Vol. I, pp. 44, 170.

whose *Elements of International Law*, published in 1836, was widely translated abroad—in French, German, Italian, Spanish, by the 1860s Chinese—and set the benchmark for definition of the discipline. Citing Grotius, Leibniz, Montesquieu and others, Wheaton explained that with few exceptions 'the public law of nations has always been, and still is, limited to the civilized and Christian people of Europe or to those of European origin'—for it was 'the progress of civilization, founded on Christianity' which had generated it.[9] By the time the first Institut de Droit International came into being, in Brussels in 1873, an association with religion was no longer required: civilization sufficed.

Classifications

This was the standard that divided the world, in a period that saw the intrusion of European imperialism, no longer into lands of weak opponents—hunter-gatherers or states without fire-arms, as in the Americas, which had occasioned the writings of Vitoria or Grotius, Locke or Vattel—but into major Asian empires and other developed states, more capable of defending themselves. This expansionist surge had already begun during the Napoleonic Wars themselves, when the British seized much of Mughal and Maratha India, and the French occupied Ottoman Egypt. But after 1815 it notably escalated, bringing the Opium Wars to China, naval penetration of Japan, conquest of Burma, Indochina and most of what is now Indonesia, not to speak of the whole littoral of North Africa, repeated invasions of Afghanistan and more.

How were these states to be classified and handled? Did they enjoy the same rights as the European powers? Tacitly, the Congress of Vienna had given its answer: barred from the Concert of Powers to which its proceedings gave birth was the Ottoman Empire, where the Concert would ultimately come to grief. That exclusion could still be referred to matters of faith. In place of this, there developed in subsequent decades the doctrine of 'the standard of civilization'. Only those states that could be regarded as civilized in European eyes were entitled to be treated on an equal footing with the powers of Europe. Just as there was now an accepted hierarchy within the comity of European nations, so the uncivilized world too was divided into different categories. Lorimer produced the most systematic theorization of this new doctrine, which became an accepted feature of writing about international law at the

---

[9] Henry Wheaton, *Elements of International Law*, London 1836, pp. 16–17, 21.

time. Three types of state failed to meet the standard of civilization. There were criminal—what today would be called outlaw or rogue—states, like the Paris Commune or fanatical Muslim societies: if Russia were to fall prey to Nihilism, it would join their ranks. There were states that did not defy civilized European norms in the same way, but—'semi-barbarous'—did not embody them either, like China or Japan. There were also states either senile or imbecile, that could not be treated as responsible agents at all—what today would be called 'failed states'. None of these categories formed part of international society proper, and the first and third required armed suppression by it—'Communism and Nihilism are forbidden by the Law of Nations', Lorimer explained. But diplomatic relations could be maintained with the second group, the semi-barbarous, provided that European powers acquired extra-territorial rights within them.[10]

Lorimer was writing on the eve of the Conference at Berlin in 1884 that settled the fate of Africa, as the Congress of Vienna had once the fate of Europe, with a vast division of colonial spoils among the assembled European states. Of these, the largest single mass of booty was acquired by the country where the emergent discipline of international law had its seat, in the form of a private company controlled by the King of Belgium. In Brussels, the Institut de Droit International celebrated the acquisi-tion, its journal declaring in 1895 that under Leopold's rule there was 'a full body of legislation whose application protects the indigenous peo-ple against all forms of oppression and exploitation'.[11] Estimates vary of the number of deaths for which its reign in the Congo was responsible: some as high as 8 to 10 million inhabitants killed.

By the turn of the century, five Asian states—China, Japan, Persia, Siam and Turkey—had graduated from semi-barbarous status to admit-tance to the first Hague Peace Conference, called by the Russian Czar in 1899, along with nineteen European countries, the United States and Mexico. Did that signify a new equality of position? At the second Hague Conference of 1907, called this time by Theodore Roosevelt, par-ticipation was enlarged to include the republics of South and Central America and the monarchies of Ethiopia and Afghanistan. The key pro-posal before the conference was the creation of an International Court of Arbitration. Who was to be represented on this? The United States and

---

[10] Lorimer, *Institutes*, pp. 123–33, 155–61.
[11] Martti Koskenniemi, *The Gentle Civilizer of Nations: The Rise and Fall of International Law 1870–1960*, Cambridge 2001, p. 160.

the major European powers took it for granted that *they* would appoint permanent members of it, other states merely rotating in temporary posts around them. To their astonishment and indignation, Brazil, in the person of the distinguished anti-slavery thinker and statesman Rui Barbosa, attacked the Anglo-German-American scheme stipulating this, declaring that it spelt 'a justice whose nature would be characterized by a juridical distinction of values between the States', ensuring that 'the Powers would then no longer be formidable only by the weight of their armies and their fleets. They would also have the superiority of right in the international magistracy, by arrogating unto themselves a privileged position in the institutions to which we pretend to entrust the meting out of justice to the nations.'[12]

Staunchly upholding the principle of the juridical equality of all sovereign states, Barbosa rallied support from what one European observer called the 'ochlocracy of smaller states'—the classical Greek term for government by the mob—to insist that the future International Court must give equal, not hierarchical, representation to the states summoned to it. Naturally, the Great Powers refused to concede this, and the Conference broke up without a result. The futility of its nominal goal of helping to secure international peace became plain seven years later, with the outbreak of the First World War.

The principle of hierarchy

At the end of the War, the victor powers England, France, Italy and the United States called the Versailles Conference to dictate terms of peace to Germany, redraw the map of Eastern Europe, divide up the Ottoman empire and—not least—create a new international body devoted to 'collective security', to ensure establishment of durable peace and justice between states, in the shape of the League of Nations. At Versailles, the United States not only made sure that Rui Barbosa was excluded from the Brazilian delegation, but that the Monroe doctrine—Washington's

---

[12] 'Hitherto, the States, however diverse because of their extent of territory, their wealth, their power, had nevertheless, among themselves, one point of moral commensuration. This was their national sovereignty. Upon this point their juridical equality could be established unshakeably. In this fortress of an equal right for all, and equally inviolable, inalienable, incontrovertible, each State, large or small, felt that it was so truly its own master and even as safe with regard to the rest, as the free citizen feels within the walls of his own house': *The Proceedings of the Hague Conferences*, Vol. II, New York 1921, pp. 645, 647.

open presumption of dominion over Latin America—was actually incorporated into the Covenant of the League as an instrument of peace. A Permanent Court of International Justice was set up in the Hague, its Article 38 continuing to invoke 'the general principles of law recognized by civilized nations'. Among those who drafted its Statutes was the author of a 600-page defence of the admirable record of Belgian administration in the Congo.

The US Senate eventually declined American entry into the League, but the design of the new organization faithfully reflected the requirements of the victor powers, since its Executive Council—the predecessor of today's UN Security Council—was controlled by the other four great powers on the winning side of the War, Britain, France, Italy and Japan, who were given exclusive permanent membership of it, on the model of the American scheme at the 1907 Hague Conference. In the face of this blatant imposition of a hierarchical order on the League, Argentina refused to take part in it from the start, and a few years later Brazil—when its demand that a Latin American country be given a permanent seat in the council was rejected—withdrew. By the end of the thirties, no less than eight other Latin American countries, large and small, had pulled out of it. Undeterred, the leading textbook of the period on international law, still widely used today, credited to Lassa Oppenheim and Hersch Lauterpacht, noted with satisfaction that 'the Great Powers are the leaders of the Family of Nations and every advance of the Law of Nations during the past has been the result of their political hegemony', which had now finally received, for the first time, in the Council of the League a formal 'legal basis and expression'.[13]

---

[13] Lassa Oppenheim, *International Law* (fifth edition), London 1937, pp. 224–25. Oppenheim, a wealthy immigrant from Hesse with a chair at Cambridge, published the first two editions of the book (1909 and 1912) before the First World War, and died in 1919, having largely completed the third (1920). By the time the fifth edition appeared in 1937, the book was no longer his. Lauterpacht, its editor, explained in his preface that he had 'deemed it proper, on many occasions, to put forward views which differ from those propounded in the former editions of this treatise'. Nowhere more so than in deleting Oppenheim's unequivocal statement, now following his original description of the Great Powers, that the League of Nations had not 'turned their political hegemony into a legal hegemony, because this preponderance is the fruit only of their political influence' (third edition, p. 200), and inserting its opposite: that the League had on the contrary given their hegemony a 'legal basis and expression' (fifth edition, p. 225). So much for philological, let alone evidential, scruple in the exposition of international law. In all subsequent editions of the treatise, Lauterpacht had become its co-author.

Lauterpacht, whose attainments are widely held to have been unsur-
passed by any international lawyer of the last century, remains a
touchstone of liberal jurisprudence in this one. He had no time for
complaints that powers like the US or UK misbehaved when it suited
them. 'Are we actually confronted', he asked of American foreign policy,
'with examples of clearly immoral conduct which will make the ordinary citizen blush?' The detachment of Panama from Colombia might
have been illegal, but could it be termed immoral? Or was it not rather
'a case in which a State, in the absence of an international legislator, has
been called upon to act as a legislator for the wider good of the international community. The issue was whether a beneficent and civilizing
enterprise should be delayed or obstructed by a State which happened
to be in possession of the territory in question.' Britain's bombardment
of Copenhagen, capital of a peaceably neutral Denmark, in 1807 and
destruction of its fleet? If 'the very existence of Great Britain was at
stake', such a sudden attack 'would not have been inconsistent either
with international law or with international morality', for 'law and mor-
als may legitimately be made to yield to the good of the international
community' (synonymous with the defeat of France).[14]

Lauterpacht would leave it to others to show 'the reasonableness and
straightforwardness' of his country's dealings with humanity at large,
adhering to principles without which 'it would cease to be part of the
civilized world'. But he could 'submit confidently that a survey of the
foreign policy of modern states will show that the immorality of international conduct is something in the nature of a myth'—a 'fiction'. Such
a verdict was not panglossian. The necessary jurisprudence had some
gaps, which needed to made good. But that was no reason for pessimism: 'international law should be regarded as incomplete and in a
state of transition to the finite and attainable ideal of a society of States
under the binding rule of law as recognized and practised by civilized
communities within their borders.'[15] The ultimate, perfectly feasible goal

---

[14] Hersch Lauterpacht, *International Law. Collected Papers. Vol II, The Law of Peace*,
Cambridge 1975, pp. 72–73, 83.
[15] Lauterpacht, *International Law. Collected Papers. Vol II*, pp. 28, 73, 75, 19. An
ardent Zionist in his youth, without in any way abandoning the cause of Israel—for
which he eventually drafted a Declaration of Independence—Lauterpacht avoided
direct involvement in political activities of any kind after he reached England in
1923. But intellectually his original concerns persisted. Around 1927 he composed a set of reflections on 'Some Biblical Problems of the Law of War', in which
he distinguished between those campaigns of the Children of Israel that were

of international law was the emergence of a supra-national Federation of the World devoted to peace. Lauterpacht's equally high-minded colleague Alfred Zimmern, another intellectual pillar of the League, was more realistic, confessing in an unguarded moment that international law was little more than 'a decorous name for the convenience of the Chancelleries', which was most useful when it 'embodied a harmonious marriage between law and force'.[16]

Words and swords

Such was the position in the inter-war period. Out of the Second World War came a new dispensation. With much of the continent in ruins, or in debt, the primacy of Europe was gone. When the United Nations was founded at San Francisco in 1945, the principle of hierarchy inherited from the League was preserved in the new Security Council, whose permanent members were given still greater powers than their predecessors in the Executive Council of old, since they now possessed rights of veto. But Western monopoly of this privilege was broken: the USSR and China were now permanent members, alongside the United States and a diminished Britain and France, and as decolonization accelerated over the next two decades, the General Assembly became a forum for resolutions and demands increasingly uncomfortable to the hegemon and its allies.

Surveying the scene in 1950, in his commanding retrospect *The Nomos of the Earth in the International Law of the Jus Publicum Europaeum*, Carl Schmitt observed that in the 19th century: 'The concept of international

---

commanded by God and those campaigns that were permitted by God. The former enjoined the extermination of all those against whom holy wars were waged—men, women and children: 'thou shalt leave nothing that breatheth'. The latter allowed, without necessarily stipulating, milder treatment. Whatever the atrocities of the first, Lauterpacht observed, they were 'religious wars of a purity unequalled in ancient times'. For in conquering Canaan, 'the Israelites went out to subdue and exterminate those peoples in the fulfilment, they believed, of God's judgement, not for selfish reasons'. The more lenient, if less codified, character of wars by permission offered a contrast whose influence, Lauterpacht mused, might be traceable in rabbinical influence on mediaeval Christian doctrines of just and unjust war. With the arrival of the League of Nations, these had now found their proper habitat in modern international law: see Hersch Lauterpacht, *International Law. Collected Papers. Vol v, Disputes, War and Neutrality*, Cambridge 2004, pp. 717–23.

[16] Alfred Zimmern, *The League of Nations and the Rule of Law (1918–1935)*, London 1977, pp. 94, 95.

law was a specifically *European* international law. This was self-evident on the European continent, especially in Germany. This was also true of such worldwide, universal concepts as *humanity, civilization* and *progress*, which determined the general concepts and theory and vocabulary of diplomats. The whole picture remained Eurocentric to the core, since by "humanity" was understood, above all, *European* humanity, civilization was self-evidently only *European* civilization, and progress was the linear development of this civilization'. But, Schmitt went on, after 1945 'Europe was no longer the sacred centre of the earth' and belief in 'civilization and progress had sunk to a mere ideological façade'. 'Today', he announced, 'the former Eurocentric order of international law is perishing. With it the old nomos of the earth, born of the fairytale-like, unexpected discovery of a New World, an unrepeatable historical event, is vanishing.'[17] International law had never been truly international. What had claimed to be universal was merely particular. What spoke in the name of humanity was empire.

After 1945, as Schmitt saw, international law ceased to be a creature of Europe. But Europe, of course, did not disappear. It simply became subsumed in another of its own overseas extensions, the United States, leaving open the question: how far has international law since 1945 remained a creature, no longer of Europe, but of the West, with at its head the American superpower? Any answer to this question refers back to another. Setting aside its historical *origins*, what is the juridical *nature* of international law as such? For its first theorists in 16th and 17th century Europe, the answer was clear. The law of nations was grounded in *natural* law, that is a set of decrees ordained by God, not to be questioned by any mortal. In other words, the Christian deity was the guarantee of the objectivity of their legal propositions.

By the 19th century, the increasing secularization of European culture gradually undermined the credibility of this religious basis for international law. In its place emerged the claim that natural law still held good, but no longer as divine commandments, rather as the expressions of a universal *human nature*, which all rational human beings could and should acknowledge. This idea, however, was soon made vulnerable in its turn by the development of anthropology and comparative sociology as disciplines, which demonstrated the enormous variety of human

---

[17] Carl Schmitt, *Der Nomos der Erde im Völkerrecht des Jus Publicum Europaeum*, Berlin 1950, pp. 199–201, 4.

customs and beliefs across history and the world, contradicting any such easy universality. But if neither the deity nor human nature could offer any secure basis for international law, how should it then be conceived?

An answer to this question could only be sought in a prior one: what was the nature of law itself? There, the greatest political thinker of the 17th—or perhaps any—century, Thomas Hobbes, had given a clear-cut answer in the Latin version of his masterpiece *Leviathan*, which appeared in 1668: *sed auctoritas non veritas facit legem*—not truth, but authority makes the law, or as he put it elsewhere: 'Covenants, without the Sword, are but Words'.[18] This would over time become known as the 'command theory of law'. That theory was the work, two centuries later, of John Austin, a clear-minded friend and follower of Bentham, who admired Hobbes above all other thinkers, and in concurring that 'every law is a command' saw what this meant for international law. His conclusion was: 'The so-called law of nations consists of opinions or sentiments current among nations generally. It therefore is *not law properly so called* . . . [for] a law set by general opinion imports the following consequences—that the party who will enforce it against any future transgressor is never determinate and assignable.'[19]

Crucial words: never determinate and assignable. Why was that so? Austin went on: 'It follows that the law obtaining between nations is not positive law; for every positive law is set by a given sovereign to a person or persons in a state of subjection to the author'—but since in a world of sovereign states 'no supreme government is in a state of subjection to another', it followed that the law of nations 'is not armed with a sanction, and does not impose a duty, in the proper acceptation of these expressions. For a sanction properly so called is an evil annexed to a command'.[20] In other words, in the absence of any determinable authority capable of either adjudicating or enforcing it, international law ceases to be law and becomes no more than opinion.

This was, and is, a conclusion deeply shocking to the liberal outlook of the overwhelming majority of today's international jurists and lawyers. What is often forgotten is that it was shared by the greatest liberal

---

[18] Thomas Hobbes, *Leviathan* (Latin text), XXVI, Oxford 2012, p. 431; (English text), XVII, p. 254.
[19] John Austin, *The Province of Jurisprudence Determined*, London 1832, p. 148.
[20] *The Province of Jurisprudence Determined*, pp. 208, 148–49.

philosopher of the 19th century, John Stuart Mill himself, who reviewed and approved Austin's lectures on jurisprudence twice. Answering attacks on the foreign policy of the short-lived French Republic in 1849, which had offered assistance to an insurgent Poland, he wrote: 'What is the law of nations? Something, which to call a law at all, is a misapplication of the term. The law of nations is simply the custom of nations'. Were these, Mill asked, 'the only kind of customs which, in an age of progress, are to be subject to no improvement? Are they alone to continue fixed, while all around them is changeable?' On the contrary, he concluded robustly, in a spirit of which Marx would have approved: 'A legislature can repeal laws, but there is no Congress of nations to set aside international customs, and no common force by which to make the decisions of such a Congress binding. The improvement of international morality can only take place by a series of violations of existing rules . . . [where] there is only a custom, the sole way of altering that is to act in opposition to it.'[21]

Doubly indeterminate

Mill was writing in a spirit of revolutionary solidarity, at a time when international law was little more than a pious phrase invoked by governments to justify whatever actions happened to suit them—it had no institutional dimension, and international lawyers did not yet exist. In the early 1880s Salisbury could still tell Parliament bluntly: 'International law has not any existence in the sense in which the term law is usually understood. It depends generally upon the prejudices of writers of textbooks. It can be enforced by no tribunal.'[22] A century later, however, institutionalization was in full flow; there was the United Nations Charter, an International Court of Justice, a body of professional lawyers and an expanding academic discipline. From the 1940s onwards, a considerable literature—Hans Kelsen and Herbert Hart the most distinguished names—sought to refute Austin by pointing out all those dimensions of law, municipal or international, that cannot be described as commands.[23]

---

[21] J. S. Mill, *Collected Works, Vol. XX*, pp. 345–46.

[22] Lord Salisbury, Speech in the House of Lords, 25 July 1887.

[23] See Hans Kelsen, *General Theory of Law and State*, Cambridge MA 1945, pp. 30–37, also 62–64, 71–74, 77–83; H. L. A. Hart, *The Concept of Law*, Oxford 1961, pp. 18–79, and on international law, pp. 208–31; (likewise, Terry Nardin, *Law, Morality and the Relations of States*, Princeton 1983, pp. 116–86). Kelsen, as might be expected, was a more careful textual scholar than Hart, engaging with Austin in a less off-hand way; but Hart's dismissal of Austin was to be more influential,

In vain, since no writer has ever been able to show that these can exempt law of a sovereign authority capable of enforcing it on penalty of infraction, as—not an exhaustive, but—always a *necessary* condition of its existence as law. All else is, as Austin put it, mere metaphor.

In the inter-war conjuncture it was once again Carl Schmitt, the antithesis of a liberal thinker, who pointed out the continuing validity of Austin's case. In a series of scathing demolitions of the pretensions of the League of Nations and its International Court, Schmitt demonstrated that the impartial rule of law they purported to uphold was invariably indeterminate, just as Austin had predicted it must be. And doubly so: indeterminate as to its *content*—as in the completely open-ended reparations imposed on Germany at Versailles, which could be adjusted by the victor powers onto the vanquished as they sought fit, pitching it into a veritable *Abgrund der Unbestimmtheit*;[24] and indeterminate—'unassignable', as Austin put it—as to its *execution*, which simply depended on the decision of the powers in command of the League of Nations and its Court. The doctrine of 'non-intervention' with which England and France ensured the victory of fascism in Spain offered another classic case of such indeterminacy, in the most eloquent illustration of Talleyrand's famous dictum that 'non-intervention is a metaphysical term that means more or less the same thing as intervention'.

---

despite the severe limitations of *The Concept of Law*, registered by his livelier colleague Brian Simpson, which were rooted in the complacent provincialism of the post-war cohort to which he belonged. Regarding himself as a philosopher, even if somewhat *manqué*, rather than a jurist, Hart lacked interest in either the history of law, the comparative study of different legal systems or even the common law of England itself, and was innocent of any experience in its enforcement. 'A lawyer who, like Hart, practised in the Chancery division, could well in the whole of his career have never seen the use of coercive violence to support the rule of law', observed Simpson. 'Consequently, Hart never gave even the simplest account of the way in which the legal order is supported by coercive force.' Human rights he ignored completely, as also Marxist or any other views of law tainted by iconoclasm—for example, that it was natural for law to 'further the interests of the dominant class, or in the global world the dominant countries, and to keep the lumpenproletariat in subjection and poverty'—when 'you have only to look around the world to see that such views cannot be rejected out of hand': A. W. Brian Simpson, *Reflections on 'The Concept of Law'*, Oxford 2004, pp. 160–64, 168, 178, 180–81. These were judgements of a friend and admirer of Hart, author of an appreciative essay about Nicola Lacey's affectionate but not uncritical life of him: 'Herbert Hart Elucidated', *Michigan Law Review*, May 2006, pp. 1437–59.
[24] Carl Schmitt, *Positionen und Begriffe im Kampf mit Weimar–Genf–Versailles. 1923–1939*, Berlin 1988, p. 3.

The essence of the international law that came into being after 1918, and with whose evolution we still live today, was what Schmitt identified as its fundamentally *discriminatory* character.[25] Wars waged by the liberal powers dominating the system were selfless police actions upholding international law. Wars waged by anyone else were criminal enterprises violating international law. What they forbade others, the liberal powers reserved the freedom to do themselves. Historically, Schmitt pointed out, the long-standing conduct of the United States in the Caribbean and Central America had pioneered this pattern.

Practice

The world in which we now live has seen a vast expansion and proliferation of what passes for international law, extending Schmitt's diagnosis in two directions. On the one hand, there has developed a category of law that is so perfect an illustration of Austin's characterization of the law of nations that he himself could scarcely have dreamt of it: the notion of a right that is not, in the technical phrase, 'justiciable'—that is, which does not even pretend to have any force of execution behind it in the real world, remaining simply a nominal aspiration—in other words, opinion pure and simple, in Austin's terms; yet which is nevertheless solemnly denominated by jurists a right. On the other hand, the number of actions taken by leading powers as they wish, either in the *name* of or in *defiance* of international law—indeterminacy without limit—has increased exponentially. Aggression is no monopoly of the hegemon. Wars of invasion have been launched without consultation, in surreptitious collusion, or outright collision, with it: England and France against Egypt, China against Vietnam, Russia against Ukraine; not to speak of lesser powers, Turkey against Cyprus, Iraq against Iran, Israel against Lebanon. None of such actions are exempt from exacting historical verdicts. That judgement, however, is necessarily political, not jural. Since 1945 wars of this order have, among the justifications alleged for them, rarely if ever (in 1956 Anglo-French attempts cut no ice in Washington) invoked international law. That is the prerogative of the hegemon and its aides in any common operation.

---

[25] Carl Schmitt, *Die Wendung zum diskriminierenden Kriegsbegriff,* Berlin 1988, p. 41 *et seq.* For Schmitt, Wilson had pioneered this innovation in the First World War. Among the leading jurists he regarded as developing it in the inter-war period were Georges Scelle of France and Lauterpacht in Britain.

A few examples will suffice. At the very foundation of the highest official embodiment of international law, namely the United Nations, whose Charter enshrines the sovereignty and integrity of its members, the United States was engaged in their systematic violation. In an Army base in the old Spanish fort a few miles from the inaugural conference that created the United Nations in San Francisco in 1945, a special team of US military intelligence was intercepting all cable traffic by delegates to their home countries; the decoded messages landed on the breakfast table of American Secretary of State Stettinius the next morning. The officer in charge of this round-the-clock operation of surveillance reported that 'the feeling in the Branch is that the success of the Conference may owe a great deal to its contribution'.[26] What did success mean here? The American historian who describes this systematic espionage exults that 'Stettinius was presiding over an enterprise his nation was already dominating and moulding'—for the UN was 'from the beginning a project of the United States, devised by the State Department, expertly guided by two hands-on Presidents, and propelled by US power . . . For a nation rightly proud of its innumerable accomplishments'—the most recent, the dropping of atomic bombs on Japan—'this unique achievement should always be at the top of its illustrious roster'.[27]

Matters were no different sixty years later. The 1946 UN Convention states that 'The premises of the UN shall be inviolable. The property and assets of the United Nations, wherever located and by whomsoever held, shall be immune from search, requisition, confiscation, expropriation and any other form of interference, whether by executive, administrative, judicial or legislative action.' In 2010 it was revealed that Clinton's wife, then Secretary of State, had directed the CIA, FBI and Secret Service to break the communication systems, appropriating passwords and encryption keys, of the Secretary-General of the UN, together with the ambassadors of all four other permanent members of the Security Council, and to secure the biometric data, credit-card numbers, email addresses and even frequent-flyer numbers of 'key UN officials, to include undersecretaries, heads of specialized agencies and chief advisers, top secretary-general aides, heads of peace operations and political field missions'.[28] Naturally,

---

[26] Stephen Schlesinger, *Act of Creation: The Founding of the United Nations*, Boulder 2003, p. 331.
[27] Schlesinger, *Act of Creation*, pp. 174, xiii.
[28] The instruction was cabled in July 2009.

neither Mrs Clinton nor the American state paid any price for their brazen violation of an international law supposedly protecting the UN itself,
the official seat of such law.

What of the international justice that international law purports to
uphold? The Tokyo Tribunal of 1946–48, organized by the United
States to try military leaders of Japan for war crimes, excluded the Showa
Emperor from the trial in order to lubricate American occupation of the
country, and treated evidence with such disregard for due process that
the Indian judge on the Tribunal, in a blistering 1,000-page condemna-
tion of it, observed that the Tokyo trials amounted to little more than
'an opportunity for the victors to retaliate', declaring 'only a lost war is a
crime'.[29] The Dutch judge on the Tribunal admitted candidly: 'Of course,
in Japan we were all aware of the bombings and the burnings of Tokyo
and Yokohama and other big cities. It was horrible that we went there for
the purpose of vindicating the laws of war, and yet saw every day how the
Allies had violated them dreadfully'[30]—Schmitt's discriminatory conception of law to the letter. The successive American wars that followed
in East Asia, first in Korea and then in Vietnam, were then littered, as
American historians have shown, with atrocities of every kind. Naturally,
no tribunal has ever held them to account.

Has anything much changed since then? In 1993 the UN Security
Council set up an International Criminal Tribunal on Yugoslavia, to
prosecute those guilty of war crimes in the break-up of the country.
Working closely with NATO, the Canadian Chief Prosecutor made sure
successful indictments for ethnic cleansing fell on Serbs, the target for
US and EU hostility, but not on Croats, armed and trained by the US
for their own operations of ethnic cleansing; and when NATO launched
its war on Serbia in 1999, excluded any of its actions—the bombing
of the Chinese Embassy in Belgrade and the rest—from her investigation of war crimes. This was perfectly logical, since as the American
press officer for NATO explained at the time: 'It was the NATO countries who established the Tribunal, who fund and support it on a daily
basis.'[31] In short, once again, the US and its allies used trials to crimi-
nalize their defeated opponents, while their own conduct remained
above judicial scrutiny.

---

[29] Radhabinod Pal, *Dissentient Judgement*, Tokyo 1999.
[30] B. V. A. Röling, *The Tokyo Trial and Beyond*, Cambridge 1993, p. 87.
[31] James Shea, 17 May 1999.

In the latest iteration of the same pattern, the now permanent International Criminal Court set up in 2002 was urged into being by the United States, which was centrally involved in its conception and preparation, but then made sure that the US would not itself be subject to the ICC's jurisdiction. When, to the great anger of the Clinton Administration, the draft Statute was changed to make possible the prosecution of members even of a state that was not a signatory to it, rendering American soldiers, pilots, torturers and others potentially vulnerable to inclusion in the mandate of the Court, the US promptly signed over a hundred bilateral agreements with countries where its military were or had been present, excluding American personnel from any such risk. Finally, in a typical farce, on his last day in the White House, Clinton instructed the US representative to sign the Statute of the future Court, knowing full well that this gesture had no chance of ratification in Congress. Naturally enough, the ICC—staffed by pliable personnel—declined to investigate any US or European actions whatever in Iraq or Afghanistan, concentrating its zeal entirely on countries in Africa, according to the unspoken maxim: one law for the rich, another for the poor.

Discriminations

As for the UN Security Council, the nominal guardian of international law, its record speaks for itself. Iraqi occupation of Kuwait in 1990 brought immediate sanctions, and a million-strong counter-invasion of Iraq. Israeli occupation of the West Bank has lasted half a century without the Security Council lifting a finger. When the US and its allies could not secure a resolution authorizing them to attack Yugoslavia in 1998–99, they used NATO instead, in patent violation of the UN Charter forbidding wars of aggression, whereupon the UN Secretary-General Kofi Annan, appointed by Washington, calmly told the world that though NATO's action might not be legal, it was legitimate—as if Schmitt had scripted his words to illustrate what he meant by the constitutive indeterminacy of international law. When, four years later, the United States and Britain launched their attack on Iraq, having had to bypass the UN Security Council under threat of a veto from France, the same Secretary-General once again blessed the operation *ex post facto*, making sure that by a unanimous vote the Security Council gave back-dated cover to Bush and Blair by voting UN assistance to their occupation of Iraq with Resolution 1483. International law may be dispensed with in launching a war; but it can always come in handy to ratify such a war after the event.

Weapons of mass destruction? The Nuclear Non-Proliferation Treaty is the starkest of all illustrations of the discriminatory character of the world order that has taken shape since the Cold War, reserving for just five powers the right to possess and deploy hydrogen bombs, and forbidding their possession to all others, who might need them more for their defence. Formally, the Treaty is not a binding rule of international law, but a voluntary agreement from which any signatory is free to withdraw. Factually, not only is a perfectly legal withdrawal from the Treaty treated as if it were a breach of international law, to be punished with the utmost severity, as in the case of North Korea, but even observance of the Treaty is open to restrictive interpretation, and if insufficiently monitored, subject to retribution, as in the case of draconian sanctions against Iran—indeterminacy and discrimination elegantly combined. That Israel has ignored the Treaty and has long possessed abundant nuclear weapons cannot be so much as mentioned. The powers punishing North Korea and Iran pretend the massive Israeli nuclear arsenal does not exist—perhaps the best commentary of all on the alchemies of international law.

Triumph of the singular

Pyongyang and Teheran are, of course, freely categorized as 'rogue' or 'pariah' states in the discourse of contemporary jural discrimination, echoing 19th-century classification of outlaw regimes.[32] Should we regard that as a stray, involuntary anachronism, like Article 38 I (c) that still sits in the Constitution of the International Court of Justice at the Hague, as reconstituted by the United Nations, continuing to announce its adherence to the principles of law that define civilized nations, in the shadow of a bust of Grotius? That would be an error. The 'standard of civilization' proclaimed—appropriately enough—in Brussels yesterday enjoys, on the contrary, a new lease of life today. We owe the first modern study of its past, *The Standard of 'Civilization' in International Society*, to an American scholar, servant of the State Department and leader of the Mormon Church, who—critical of its use to justify colonial excesses in times gone

---

[32] For the history and contemporary currency of these notions, see the outstanding study by Gerry Simpson, *Great Powers and Outlaw States: Unequal Sovereigns in the International Legal Order*, Cambridge 2004, passim.

by—noted, nevertheless, the elevating role it could also play in educating non-Europeans to higher codes of moral conduct, and commended two possible successors to it: a new 'standard of human rights' being pioneered by Europeans, or alternatively a 'standard of modernity', bringing the blessings of civilization in the shape of cosmopolitan culture to all.[33]

That was in 1984. He was prescient. In the new century, the holder of a chair in a school named after the mentor of former Secretary of State Condoleezza Rice, explaining that 'something like a new standard of civilization is needed to save us from the barbarity of a pristine sovereignty', proclaims human rights—above all as practised by the European Union—as that standard; and a principal offender against it, the Palestinian Authority.[34] Alternatively, a leading American specialist in terrorism and cybersecurity offers a more palpable updating of the notion. Structural Adjustment Plans imposed on underdeveloped countries by the IMF are the contemporary equivalent of the enlightened capitulations of old that helped to bring Ottomans and others into the comity of acceptable states, continuing their work of 'civilizational harmonization', essential to international society.[35] More ambitiously still, an Iranian scholar from Denmark, denouncing Islam as an Oriental totalitarianism, has announced the arrival of a Global Standard of Civilization—GSC—as the lodestar of humanity's advance to a better world, gaining momentum every day. We are living, he exclaims, a new 'Grotian moment', in which the two pillars of global civilization are 'capitalism and liberalism'.[36] Nor have historians been found wanting. The most prominent, and prolific, contemporary historian at Harvard, Niall Ferguson, author of works on the Rothschild and Warburg banks, the First and Second World Wars and the history of money, restores the singular with unruffled aplomb in *Civilization: The West and the Rest* (2011), devoted to an explanation of all the reasons why the former triumphed over the latter.

---

[33] Gerrit Gong, *The Standard of 'Civilization' in International Society*, Oxford 1984, pp. 91–93.
[34] Jack Donnelly, 'Human Rights: A New Standard of Civilization?', *International Affairs*, vol. 74, no. 1, 1998, pp. 1–23.
[35] David Fidler, 'A Kinder, Gentler System or Capitulations? International Law, Structural Adjustment Policies and the Standard of Liberal, Globalized Civilization', *Texas International Law Journal*, vol. 35, January 2000, pp. 387–414.
[36] Mehdi Mozaffari, 'The Transformationalist Perspective and the Rise of a Global Standard of Civilization', *International Relations of the Asia–Pacific*, vol. 1, no. 2, 2001, pp. 259, 262.

Writing at the turn of the sixties, Braudel reiterated Febvre's conviction that Valéry was wrong: 'Civilizations are a reality of very long duration. They are not "mortal", above all—despite Valéry's too famous phrase—as measured by our individual lives. Lethal accidents . . . occur to them far less often than we think. In many cases, they are merely sent to sleep.' Customarily, it is only 'their most exquisite flowers, their rarest achievements, that perish, but their deep roots survive many a rupture, many a winter.'[37] There might be 'an inflation of civilization in the singular', but 'it would be puerile to imagine this, beyond its triumph, doing away with the different civilizations that are the real personages who still confront us'. Characteristically, however, Braudel's conclusions oscillated. In one register, the singular and plural collaborate fruitfully: 'Plural and singular form a dialogue, complementing each other and differentiating themselves from one another, sometimes visible to the naked eye, almost without requiring attention.' On the next page, a very different note is struck: 'A blind, ferocious struggle is at work under various names, and on various fronts, between civilizations and civilization. The task is to tame, to channel it, to impose a new humanism on it', and 'in that battle without precedent many cultural structures can crack and all of them at once'.[38] Half a century later, we may ask, has civilization in the singular been subdued by civilizations in the plural, as he hoped it would be?

The spectacle of international law suggests otherwise. Braudel had a wide and deep comparative grasp of the material and cultural dynamics of human history, giving him an unrivalled sense of the differences between civilizations. Much less interested in their political and ideological dimensions, he identified civilization in the singular—*scilicet* Western civilization—too simply with just that of 'the machine': essentially, technology, which he rightly thought could be adapted by any of the civilizations of the world that had survived to the present. Of the power of the intellectual and institutional order of the West, not to speak of its military predominance, he took less account.

The force of opinion

None of this, of course, means that international law is without any substance that can for practical purposes be regarded as universal. It

---

[37] Fernand Braudel, 'L'Apport de l'histoire des civilisations', in Gaston Berger, ed., *Encyclopédie française, Vol. XX, Le Monde en devenir*, Paris 1959, 12: 10.

[38] Braudel, 'L'Apport de l'histoire des civilisations', 12: 12–13.

is enough to consider the fact that no state in the world dispenses with appeals to it, if only because all benefit from at least one convention associated with it: the diplomatic immunity of their embassies abroad, respected even after war has been declared by the host country against the state they represent—what might be called the Minimum Content of International Law, by analogy with Hart's reduction to the same of Natural Law. Needless to say, every embassy of a major state, and most of lesser ones, is crammed with personnel engaged full-time in espionage, with no legal warrant in international law. Little comfort for its theorists is to be found in such incongruities.

To conclude: on any realistic assessment, international law is neither truthfully international nor genuinely law. That, however, does not mean it is not a force to be reckoned with. It is a major one. But its reality is as Austin described it: what in the vocabulary which he inherited from Hobbes he termed opinion, and today we would call ideology. There, as an ideological force in the world at the service of the hegemon and its allies, it is a formidable instrument of power. For Hobbes, opinion was the key to the political stability or instability of a kingdom. As he wrote: 'The actions of men proceed from their opinions, and in the well governing of opinions consisteth the well governing of men's actions'—thus 'the power of the mighty hath no foundation but in the opinion and belief of the people'.[39] It was seditious opinions, he believed, that triggered the Civil War in England, and it was to instill correct opinions that he wrote *Leviathan*, which he hoped would be taught in the universities that were 'the fountains of civil and moral doctrine', to bring 'public tranquility' back to the land.[40] We do not have to share the extent of Hobbes's respect for the power of opinion, or indeed his preferences among the opinions of his day, to acknowledge the validity of the importance he attached to them. International law may be a mystification. It is not a trifle.

How then should it be conceived? For the most formidable of international jurists today, the Finnish scholar Martti Koskenniemi, international law is best termed a hegemonic technique, in the Gramscian sense. For Gramsci, he notes, the exercise of hegemony always involved the successful representation of a particular interest as a universal value. That, certainly, the standard of civilization attempted, and in its heyday achieved, as the vocabulary of the 'international community' has

---

[39] Hobbes, *Leviathan* (English text), XVIII, p. 272; *Behemoth*, p. 16.
[40] Hobbes, *Leviathan*, 'A Review and Conclusion', p. 1140.

typically done since. International law in that sense had never ceased to be an instrument of Euro-American power. But just because it offered an ostensibly universal discourse, it was open to appropriation and reversal, claiming it for other, wider and more humane interests.[41] Even at the height of imperial hubris in the 19th century, after all, eloquent voices had resisted the standard of civilization: 'The argument employed in our time . . . to justify and disguise the spoliation of weaker races is no longer the call of religion, but of civilization: modern peoples have a civilizing mission to fulfill they cannot decline', wrote a modest lawyer from Bordeaux, Charles Salomon in 1889. More radical even than Braudel, he went on: 'There is talk of civilization as if there were an absolute of just one: those who do so all believe they are entitled to the first rank of it. Changing Joseph de Maistre's well-known dictum slightly, we might well say: I know of civilizations, I know nothing of civilization.'[42]

Modern international law is thus, as Koskenniemi observes, intrinsically threaded with contestation, and as its contemporary instrumentation for the will of today's hegemon and its satellites has grown ever more brazen, so the number of critical legal minds not only questioning but seeking to reverse its imperial use has grown too. The most lucid do so without attributing more strength to its claims than they can bear. In the *mot* of a distinguished French jurist, international law is 'performative'. That is, such pronouncements in its name seek to bring into being what they invoke, rather than refer to any existent reality, however laudable.[43]

The same dialectic, of course, has more famously been true of municipal law, invoked in Europe at least since the 17th century in defence of the weak against the strong, who created it. But there Austin's axiom makes the difference. Within the nation-states, as they became, of Europe, there was always a determinable sovereign authorized to enforce the law, and as this authority passed from crowns to peoples, not coincidentally came also the legitimate power to change it. In relations between states, unlike relations among citizens, neither condition holds. So while hegemony

---

[41] Martti Koskenniemi, 'International Law and Hegemony: a Reconfiguration', in *The Politics of International Law*, Oxford 2011, pp. 221–22 *et seq.*

[42] Charles Salomon, *L'Occupation des territoires sans maître: Étude de droit international*, Paris 1889, pp. 193, 195.

[43] The adjective, and what it designates, was regarded by Hart as happiest of all the *trouvailles* of J. L. Austin, the analytic philosopher of whom he was an adept in Oxford.

functions in both national and international arenas, and by definition always combines coercion and consent, on the international plane coercion is for the most part *legibus solutus* and what consent is secured inevitably weaker and more precarious. International law operates to hide that gap. Koskenniemi began his career with a brilliant demonstration of the two poles between which the structure of international legal argument had historically moved, entitled *From Apology to Utopia*: either international law supplied servile pretexts for whatever actions states wished to take, or it purveyed a lofty moral vision of itself as, in Hooker's words, 'her voice the harmony of the world', with no relation to any empirical reality. What Koskenniemi failed to see was the interlocking of the two: not utopia *or* apology, but utopia *as* apology: responsibility to protect as charter for the destruction of Libya, preservation of peace for the strangulation of Iran, and the rest.

Still, defenders of international law can argue that its existence, however often it is abused by states in practice, is at least better than would be its absence, invoking in their aid La Rochefoucauld's well-known maxim: *L'hypocrisie est un hommage que le vice rend à la vertu*. Yet critics can equally reply that here it should be reversed. Ought it not rather to read: hypocrisy is the counterfeit of virtue by vice, the better to conceal vicious ends: the arbitrary exercise of power by the strong over the weak, the ruthless prosecution or provocation of war in the philanthropic name of peace?

independent thinking from polity

Migration as Economic Imperialism
How International Labour Mobility Undermines Economic Development in Poor Countries
Immanuel Ness

In this sharp corrective to conventional wisdom, Ness asserts that remittances do not bring growth to poor countries but extend national dependence on the export of migrant workers, leading to warped and unequal development on the global periphery.

July 2023 | PB: 978-1-5095-5399-0 | £18.99

After Nativism
Belonging in an Age of Intolerance
Ash Amin

The lines drawn by nativism are of an affective nature about imagined community, with meanings of belonging and voice lying at the heart of popular perceptions of just dues. This is the territory that progressive forces need to reclaim in order to shift public sentiment away from xenophobic intolerance.

Sept 2023 | PB: 978-1-5095-5731-8 | £15.99

In a Human Voice
Carol Gilligan

Forty years after her landmark book, *In a Different Voice*, Gilligan returns to the subject matter of her classic book, re-examining its central arguments and concerns from the vantage point of the present.

Sept 2023 | PB: 978-1-5095-5679-3 | £12.99

The Future of Foreign Policy Is Feminist
Kristina Lunz
Translated by Nicola Barfoot

This is nothing less than an inclusive, visionary policy for the twenty-first century, one where security and prosperity, health and climate justice are possible – in other words: where peace is possible for everyone, everywhere.

Sept 2023 | HB: 978-1-5095-5783-7 | £25.00

Also a History of Philosophy, Volume 1
The Project of a Genealogy of Postmetaphysical Thinking
Jürgen Habermas
Translated by Ciaran Cronin

This is the first volume of a ground-breaking new work by Jürgen Habermas on the history of philosophy. In this major new work, Habermas sets out the ideas that inform his systematic account of the history of Western philosophy as a genealogy of postmetaphysical thinking.

Sept 2023 | HB: 978-1-5095-4389-2 | £35.00

CAITLÍN DOHERTY

TOPOGRAPHIES OF CAPITAL

Gender, Class and Nature in Fraser's Critical Theory

TODAY, NANCY FRASER may fairly be called the leading social-ist feminist of the Anglophone world. Emerging from a background in social philosophy and critical theory, she has produced a body of thought as striking for its radical, totalizing ambitions as for its conceptual clarity and lucid exposition, and impressive not least for its consistent development, in continuous engagement with historical reality. The critiques of French post-structuralism, American pragmatism and latter-day Frankfurt School theory in *Unruly Practices* (1989), where Fraser first developed her concept of a gendered politics of need; the landmark exchanges with Judith Butler, Seyla Benhabib and Drucilla Cornell over the 'linguistic turn' in *Feminist Contentions* (1995); the sophisticated critique of a politics limited to affirmative-action and cultural-difference agendas in *Justice Interruptus* (1997); the debate—which Fraser very much gets the better of—with Axel Honneth in *Redistribution or Recognition?* (2003); the expansion of notions of representation, redistribution and recognition to the trans-national level in *Scales of Justice* (2008), calling for a voice for the global poor in the aftermath of the US invasions of Afghanistan and Iraq; the watershed critique of neoliberal 'progressivism' in *Fortunes of Feminism* (2013); the path-breaking analysis of the combined economic, political and ecological crisis that has unfolded over the past decade, in *The Old Is Dying* (2019) and Fraser's latest book, *Cannibal Capitalism* (2022)—the range, depth and vitality of this work speaks for itself.

In the course of this, Fraser has managed to combine a high-level international teaching career—as Loeb professor of politics and phi-losophy at the New School, with visiting professorships *inter alia* in

Paris, Frankfurt, Amsterdam, Berlin, Vienna, Cambridge—with unfailing radical commitment. Again and again, she has been to the left of prevailing intellectual wisdom: insisting on economic as well as cultural critique at the height of the post-structuralism boom; breaking decisively with Clintonite feminism; arguing against the inequities of financialized capitalism—the younger generations reeling from 'crushing debt, precarious work, besieged livelihoods, dwindling services, crumbling infrastructures, hardened borders, racialized violence, deadly pandemics, extreme weather and overarching political dysfunctions', as she puts it.[1]

At the same time, Fraser's literary and intellectual approach is an unusual one for the left. Trained in analytic philosophy, her method involves positing sets of conceptual distinctions, whose logics she then unfolds. Often these categories are shorthand terms for complex strategic perspectives or political-philosophical ideas: 'justice', with its Rawlsian ring; 'recognition' and 'redistribution'; the domains of 'the cultural' and 'the economic'. They are related to each other through elegant geometries, generating further abstractions—ideal-types, paradigms, modes, remedies, claims. As Fraser has argued: 'Only by abstracting from the complexities of the real world can we devise a conceptual schema that can illuminate it'—'for heuristic purposes, analytical distinctions are indispensable.'[2] On the left, however, there is often an instinctive sense—not ungrounded—that analytic philosophy is an alien form. Critics have argued that Fraser's categories are *too* abstract; that she does not engage sufficiently with the historical and empirical complexities of her subject matter.[3] This essay, though, is interested instead in what

---

[1] Nancy Fraser, *Cannibal Capitalism: How Our System Is Devouring Democracy, Care and the Planet—And What We Can Do About It*, London and New York 2022, p. xiii; henceforth CC.

[2] Nancy Fraser, 'From Redistribution to Recognition? Dilemmas of Justice in a "Post-Socialist" Age', NLR 1/212, July–Aug 1995, p. 70.

[3] Fraser herself has some sympathy with this perspective. In a footnote on 'class', explaining that for purposes of analytical contrast she is using the term in a 'highly stylized, orthodox and theoretical way', she acknowledges that in other contexts she herself would prefer a fuller interpretation that gave more weight to the cultural, historical and discursive dimensions of 'class' explored by Edward Thompson or Joan Wallach Scott: Fraser, 'From Redistribution to Recognition?', p. 75, n. 15. For representative samples of critics demanding more empirical evaluation, see Hester Eisenstein's review of *Fortunes of Feminism* in *Science & Society*, vol. 80, no. 3, July 2016, or Nanette Funk, 'Contra Fraser on Feminism and Neoliberalism', *Hypatia*, vol. 28, no. 1, Winter 2013.

her heuristics have to tell us about capitalism itself and the interrelation of its economic, social, geopolitical and environmental crises. First it is necessary to trace the development of her approach.

Making of a feminist philosopher

Fraser was born in Baltimore in 1947. Her father, a second-generation immigrant of Lithuanian Jewish descent, was an importer of kidskin gloves; her mother was from a mixed family, part Russian-Jewish, part Irish Catholic, long-settled on Maryland's poor agricultural shore; both were 'FDR liberals'. A precocious student, Fraser was frustrated with the limits of a 'middling' public-school education and won a place to study classics at Bryn Mawr, where she discovered a passion and aptitude for philosophy. Caught up in the ferment of the civil-rights movement, then the protests against the war in Vietnam, she joined the SDS Labor Committee and was a full-time militant for five years following graduation. Going back to school in 1974, after the movement had wound down, to begin doctoral work on continental philosophy at CUNY, this activist experience distinguished her from her younger peers among critical-theory students, who had come of age amid the political confusions of the Ford–Carter years and were keen to do away with what, for them, were the exclusionary grand narratives of class dialectics. Fraser, too, was enthused by the energies of the new movements and the post-structural revolution, but always adopted a 'both/and' approach: discourse theory *and* Marx, Habermas *and* feminism.

The argumentative structure of her doctoral thesis set the template.[4] Taking a group of texts—Tocqueville's *Recollections*, Victor Hugo's *Napoleon the Little*, Flaubert's *Sentimental Education*, Marx's *Eighteenth Brumaire*—Fraser set out to determine a means of adjudicating between 'competing descriptions of social reality', in this case, that of the revolutionary year of 1848. Faced with a choice between the critical, the empirical and the narrative, she concluded that the three dimensions were not independent: rather, 'each presupposes the others and none is foundational with respect to the others.' Visible already in this early work were two defining traits of Fraser's philosophical approach: a tendency to transcend dualisms by the addition of a third category that

---

[4] Nancy Fraser, *Adjudicating Between Competing Social Descriptions: The Critical, Empirical and Narrative Dimensions (With an Application to Marxism)*, PhD Thesis, City University of New York 1980.

mediates between the assumed opposition, while corresponding to, or overlapping with, elements of each group; and a rejection of any hierarchy of causation in favour of a pluralistic descriptive method, shifting in response to the social reality it encounters. Typically, she would distinguish analytically clear categorizations and then apply a dialectical logic to describe the complex imbrication of social kinds, with a view to uncovering an emancipatory dynamic.

Descriptive sensitivity formed the heart of Fraser's critique of Jürgen Habermas in a germinal 1985 essay, 'What's Critical About Critical Theory?'.[5] Her starting point was the young Marx's definition of critical theory as the 'self-clarification of the struggles of the age': if those struggles included women's fight for liberation, then a critical theory worthy of the name should shed light on the structures of oppressive gender relations and the prospects of the feminist movement. Examined in that light, Habermas's construction fell short. Fraser was entirely at home amid the sometimes bafflingly technical terminology of the three-volume *Theory of Communicative Action*, handling its models with confidence. As a young feminist philosopher, she found much that was helpful in Habermas's critique of the advanced-capitalist welfare-state societies of the 'long upturn'. But where Habermas drew a sharp, though layered, distinction between an exploitative system and an innocent lifeworld, Fraser used the gendering of domestic labour, waged work and political participation to demonstrate the complex inter-relations of domination and family life. Habermas's androcentric view of the nuclear family and failure to theorize the gendered dimension of social power risked eclipsing the positive and useful aspects of his thought, Fraser argued: his interpretive view of human needs, his distinction between 'normatively secured' and 'communicatively achieved' action contexts, his four-term model of public/private relations.[6]

Beyond her political commitment to women's liberation, Fraser's designation as a feminist philosopher is attributable not so much to a strong engagement with the corpus of feminist writing, contemporary or historic, but to the centrality of domestic labour, welfare and the economic role of the family in her social theory, which places the 'woman

---

[5] 'What's Critical about Critical Theory? The Case of Habermas and Gender', *New German Critique*, vol. 44, no. 1, Spring-Summer 1985.
[6] *Unruly Practices: Power, Discourse and Gender in Contemporary Social Theory*, Cambridge 1989.

question' at the heart of her discussions of economic redistribution and identity recognition. The worsening position of women, especially black women, affected by the welfare cuts of the Clinton era, at a time of soaring asset wealth, drove the production of 'Genealogy of Dependency', a paper co-written with Linda Gordon, and the programmatic 'After the Family Wage', a thought experiment about emancipatory models of social reproduction that would help to deconstruct gender. Fraser's canonical text, 'From Redistribution to Recognition?', grew out of this 1990s experience. Demands for the recognition of gender, ethnic, racial and sexual differences were being forwarded in a world of worsening material inequality, environmental toxicity, falling life-expectancy rates. Justice required both recognition and redistribution, Fraser argued, as well as theorization of the relations between them. Focusing on 'race' (already scare-quoted in 1995) and gender, she contrasted 'transformative' programmes—the deep restructuring of relations of production and the deconstruction of underlying cultural-valuation dichotomies of 'race' and gender—to 'affirmative' ones: mainstream multiculturalism, affirmative action and welfare-state amelioration of inequalities within the existing economic and cultural system.

Fraser's refusal to prioritize norms and values over material determinants provoked a stinging response from Judith Butler entitled 'Merely Cultural'—not an expression that Fraser herself had ever used. Fraser agreed with Butler that 'the need to speak as and for *women*' had to 'be reconciled with the complementary necessity of continually contesting the word.' But she opposed the uncritical celebration of 'differences' among women and the failure to confront real conflicts of interest between them. She argued that the conjuncture urgently required the 'harmonization' of claims from social movements for recognition with those of class-based organizations struggling on the terrain of economic redistribution.[7] A few years later, Fraser reiterated her belief in the interdependence of the subjective and objective, in an exchange with Axel Honneth: 'distribution and recognition do not occupy separate spheres. Rather, they interpenetrate to produce complex patterns of

---

[7] Judith Butler, 'Merely Cultural', NLR 1/227, Jan–Feb 1998; Nancy Fraser, 'Heterosexism, Misrecognition and Capitalism: A Response to Judith Butler', NLR 1/228, Mar–April 1997; see also Anne Philips, 'From Inequality to Difference: A Severe Case of Displacement?', NLR 1/224, July–Aug 1997. Many of the engagements of this period are collected in the volume *Adding Insult to Injury: Nancy Fraser Debates Her Critics*, ed. Kevin Olson, London and New York 2008.

subordination . . . It follows that distribution and recognition can never be fully disentangled. All interactions partake simultaneously of both dimensions, albeit in different proportions.'[8]

Crisis era

The major staging-posts of Fraser's thinking from the 1980s through to the watershed of the 2008–09 financial crisis are helpfully collected in *Fortunes of Feminism*, whose Prologue retrospectively presents the story of American gender politics over this period as 'a drama in three acts'.[9] In Act One, an insurrectionary women's liberation movement emerged from the ferment of the New Left and joined with other radical currents in an attempt to overthrow technocratic Fordist capitalism. In Act Two, as utopian energies ebbed, feminism was drawn into the orbit of identity politics, just as a rising neoliberalism 'declared war on social equality'. Fraser settled accounts with the business-friendly feminism epitomized by Hillary Clinton in the 2009 essay, 'Feminism, Capitalism and the Cunning of History'. In Act Three, just starting to unfold within the trough of the Great Recession, her hope was that feminism might regain its rebel spirit, while deepening its signature insights—'its structural critique of capitalism's androcentrism, its systemic analysis of male domination and its gender-sensitive revisions of democracy and justice.'[10]

Since then, Fraser has responded to the successive waves of struggles—environmental protests, Black Lives Matter, strikes, #MeToo, abortion rights—with a wide-ranging research project, developed in lecture series, seminars and essays, and now collected in two complementary books,

---

[8] Nancy Fraser and Axel Honneth, *Redistribution or Recognition: A Political–Philosophical Exchange*, London and New York 2004, p. 217. There are parallels here with Fraser's later critique of Polanyi, whose idealized view of 'society', moving to heal the wounds inflicted by the *laissez-faire* 'market', needed to be complicated by the dynamics of a third current, 'emancipation', alternately allied with the two other strands: Fraser, 'A Triple Movement? Parsing the Crisis of Politics After Polanyi', NLR 91, May–June 2013.

[9] Nancy Fraser, *Fortunes of Feminism: From State-Managed Capitalism to Neoliberal Crisis*, London and New York, 2013, pp. 1–16.

[10] Nancy Fraser, 'Feminism, Capitalism and the Cunning of History', NLR 56, March–April 2009, collected in *Fortunes of Feminism*; the quotation is from the volume's Prologue, p. 1.

Cannibal Capitalism and *Capitalism: A Conversation in Critical Theory*.[11] In this work, the capitalist social formation has become the explicit foreground, 'the direct object of critique'. Her ambitions are political as well as theoretical: to conceptualize a crisis in which global warming, social breakdown, economic stagnation and political atomization are entwined, while also limning out a counter-hegemonic project sufficiently broad to coordinate the diffuse struggles the conjuncture has provoked. The types of practical and applied conclusions she suggests have also been radicalized over the past decade: from determining 'just' outcomes to inspiring political action aimed at dismantling capitalism *in toto*.

Read together, *Capitalism: A Conversation in Critical Theory*—an extended dialogue between Fraser and the Frankfurt-trained social philosopher Rahel Jaeggi—and the more popular *Cannibal Capitalism* in turn expound and systematize Fraser's argument for an expanded concept of capitalism. Fraser's premise is that an understanding of the present crisis cannot be restricted to economic questions alone. She sets out to reveal the imbrication—a crucial term for her work—of the economic and the political, social and environmental dimensions of the crisis, writing for younger generations who had grown up without access to earlier critiques of capitalism, and for older readers who had never really integrated issues of gender, 'race' and ecology into their analysis.

In *Cannibal Capitalism*, a renewed *Kapitalkritik* necessitates a return to Marx, from whom Fraser borrows both a classical definition of the capitalist economy—defined by private ownership of the means of production, wage labour as the general means of subsistence and a competitive dynamic of accumulation—and the broader concept of capitalism as a social order. Methodologically, her starting point is that of *Capital*, Volume One, which progresses, she argues, by a series of epistemic shifts to reveal the 'background conditions' of capitalist accumulation. Marx begins, with his discussion of the commodity form, from the bourgeois standpoint of the sphere of circulation, the exchange of equivalents; but he soon shifts to a deeper perspective, that of the 'hidden abode of production', where capital accumulates not through

---

[11] Nancy Fraser and Rahel Jaeggi, *Capitalism: A Conversation in Critical Theory*, London and New York 2023 [2018]; henceforth, C:ACCT. Jaeggi, a former researcher for Axel Honneth, teaches social philosophy at the Humboldt and is the author *inter alia* of *Critique of Forms of Life* (2018).

equal exchange but exploitation—the non-compensation of a portion of a worker's labour time, legally sanctioned by the labour contract. Finally, with another 'equally momentous' shift in standpoint, he reveals the background condition of production and exploitation to be primitive accumulation—an overtly brutal process of expropriation with no pretence of equal exchange.

Fraser's move is to orchestrate further epistemic shifts, to help us see other background conditions for capital accumulation, this time in the non-economic realms—public authority, social reproduction, the natural world—on which capital depends. Or, as she puts it to Jaeggi, to take the Marxian method of looking 'beneath' a given socio-historical complex for its underlying conditions of possibility and apply it more widely. These non-economic zones are at once the overlooked 'backstories' to classically defined economic activity and sites for 'emancipatory currents of critical theorizing', whose lessons must be incorporated with those of Marx.[12] The central argument, developed thematically, is that activities performed in the 'background' should not be seen as secondary, but understood as essential features of the system. Capitalism entails not only the economic realm but the divisions of the world to which imperialist expropriations have given rise; the totality of un-waged work and the social reproduction of labour; the spoliation of non-human nature; and the political authority on which the extraction and circulation of profit depend—'hidden abodes', to which four central chapters of *Cannibal Capitalism* correspond.

Fraser has explained that she sees each of these background zones as arising concurrently with the capitalist economy, co-constituted by the rupture it imposed on a pre-existing unity.[13] Thus, economic and political power had been fused in the figure of the feudal lord, who both expropriated the harvest and imposed his law; the advent of capitalism brought the separation of the economic and political spheres, the border between them constituting a zone of conflict. Similarly, in pre-capitalist subsistence societies, processes of production and social reproduction had formed a continuum, but capitalist industrial production established the domestic sphere as its other, giving pre-existing gender divisions a sharper modern form. Brute expropriation, not least in the world regions colonized by capitalist powers, imposed another

---

[12] C:ACCT, pp. 30–31.   [13] C:ACCT, pp. 62–63.

structural division between exploited workers in the capitalist heartlands and expropriable others; again, Fraser argues, whatever earlier forms of xenophobic prejudice may have existed, racial difference was given its modern guise through capitalism's separation of the expropriated and the exploited. Likewise, capitalist production instituted a 'metabolic rift' in relation to the natural world, another contested division.

A central goal of *Cannibal Capitalism* is to illuminate the ways in which these background realms interrelate with the economic foreground and with each other, feeding into a broader crisis of capitalist society. Yet capitalism's dynamism, its restless expansionism and constant overshooting of state borders mean that Fraser's structural analysis must also be periodized historically and placed in a world perspective. Adapting Immanuel Wallerstein's world-system 'epochs', Fraser defines four 'regimes of accumulation': mercantile capitalism, roughly the sixteenth to eighteenth centuries; the liberal-colonialist, *laissez-faire* capitalism of the long nineteenth century; the Keynesian or 'state-managed' post-war regime; and the neoliberal era of credit-fuelled financialized capitalism. How do the broader dimensions of capitalist society—social-reproductive, environmental, political—articulate with capital's drive for accumulation across these successive regimes?

Production and reproduction

Fraser begins with two core capitalist dynamics: exploitation, through waged labour, and expropriation—the confiscation of natural resources and human capabilities, conscripted into the circuits of capitalist expansion. In the mercantile era, European expropriations proceeded both in the conquered and colonized lands of the New World, Africa and southern Asia, and—with the English enclosures and Scottish clearances—at home. Under the liberal-colonial regime, the growth of capitalist industry produced an exploited proletariat in the metropolitan centres, which gradually won the right to citizenship, suffrage and legal protections; this sharpened—and decisively racialized—the distinctions between exploitation and expropriation, which now mapped onto different world regions. Under the imperialist-capitalist world system, the two became mutually constitutive and tightly entwined: the exploited US citizen-worker acquired an aura of freedom by comparison to expropriated indigenous groups or chattel slaves. Globally, too, the distinction correlated 'roughly but unmistakably' with what DuBois called 'the colour line'.[14] The stark opposition between exploitation and expropriation began to weaken in the post-war period, under the impact of decolonization and civil rights. With the advent of financialized capitalism, Fraser argues, it underwent new shifts. Forms of debt-based expropriation expanded across the world, while manufacturing shifted to the South and East; former industrial workers in the advanced-capitalist countries were stripped of their relative privilege, amid falling real wages and rising household debt. The relation now was more of a continuum—a racialized spectrum of exploited-expropriated citizen-workers.[15]

Capitalism was always 'deeply entangled' with racial oppression, Fraser writes; the choice of verb allows her to unfold a continuous yet malleable historical relationship between shifting ethnic and phenotypical designations and dynamic socio-economic practices—from eighteenth-century slave plantations to multinational corporations, persisting into the 'deindustrializing, subprime, mass-incarceration' present. But if the structuring exploitation-expropriation division of populations that underwrote racialization is disappearing, might that entanglement start to prove contingent—a lingering residue of capitalism's history that no longer plays any real purpose? Is a non-racial capitalism now possible? Though no longer strictly 'necessary' to it, racial antagonisms are on the rise, Fraser notes. The financialized regime of accumulation generates intense insecurities and paranoias; the grievances of formerly 'protected' workers are more likely to find far-right expression—a toxic combination of 'sedimented dispositions, exacerbated anxieties, cynical manipulations'—faced with progressive neoliberal elites appealing to 'fairness' while subjecting them to redundancies and debt. A 'non-racial' capitalism based on ballooning inequality would still leave most in miserable conditions. A more transformative approach would aim to build a cross-racial alliance to eradicate both exploitation and expropriation—however far off that may seem at present.[16]

Fraser turns next to what she terms the 'crisis of care', expressed through social exhaustion and time poverty, as the energies needed for human replenishment are sapped by neoliberalism's economic pressures. The

---

[14] Fraser acknowledges that historical realities were more mixed: there were subproletarian populations in the metropolitan centres, where the ranks of 'protected' workers were at first restricted to the so-called aristocracy of labour, just as there were waged workers in the colonies and peripheral zones: CC, p. 43.
[15] CC, pp. 27–47.   [16] CC, pp. 48–52.

'care' strand is so central to the broader crisis that none of the other strands can be understood without it, she writes. But the converse was also true: the social-reproduction crisis cannot be understood on its own. It needs to be grasped as an acute expression of an inherent contradiction under capitalism, taking varied forms in different epochs. The drive for accumulation continually cannibalizes the partially non-market activities on which capital relies for the reproduction of the labour force. Historically, this process began with the early industrial revolution, when women and children were dragooned into the factory—capital 'plundering' the domain of social reproduction, stretching the capacity for sustenance to breaking point. Middle-class moral panic and reformist labour organizing led eventually to 'protective' legislation, excluding women from the workplace, and a new gender imaginary of domesticity and female dependence—in the metropolitan core, the zone of exploitation. In the colonial world, the zone of expropriation, the ravaging of indigenous social-reproductive relations continued unchecked.[17]

In Fraser's telling, the post-war Keynesian regime of accumulation forged a novel synthesis of marketization with social protection—Polanyi's opposites[18]—which aimed to stabilize the economy-reproduction boundary under the high-wage, high-consumption Fordist model, based on the ideal of the male breadwinner and female housewife. Yet 'housewifization' denied the third key movement, emancipation, which Fraser insists should be added to Polanyi's matrix. From the 1970s, as both feminist critique and neoliberal assaults helped to weaken the case for social protectionism (never idealized by Fraser), these distinctions were re-forged. Under the emerging financialized-capitalist regime, emancipation was paired with marketization as a new form of progressive neoliberalism. Recruiting women into paid work while slashing funds for social provision, this forced further responsibilities for care onto households while diminishing their capacity to provide it:

> The logic of economic production overrides that of social reproduction, destabilizing the very processes on which capital depends—compromising the social capacities, both domestic and public, that are needed to sustain accumulation over the long term. Destroying its own conditions of possibility, capital's accumulation dynamic mimics the ouroboros and eats its own tail.[19]

---

[17] CC, pp. 53–62.
[18] Fraser, 'A Triple Movement?'.
[19] CC, pp. 57–8.

The resulting crisis, Fraser argues, has produced an upsurge of 'boundary struggles', calling for public support around social-reproductive issues—healthcare, food security, parental leave. Yet if the root of the care crisis lies in capitalism's social contradiction, it will not be resolved by policy tinkering. A deeper transformation is required, 'reinventing the production/reproduction distinction and reimagining the gender order' in ways that ensure both social protection and emancipation.[20]

Nature and power

Turning to nature, *Cannibal Capitalism* finds another domain in which the regime of accumulation is devouring its own conditions of existence. Yet if there is a growing consensus that global warming constitutes an urgent threat, there is no agreement on what structural forces are driving the process nor on what type of societal change is required to alter course. Fraser argues that the relation between capital and nature is inherently crisis prone: capitalist production depends on nature as a source of raw materials and a sink for waste—yet it also posits a stark divide between the realm of the economy, as a field of human action, and that of nature as the realm of unthinking 'stuff'. Capital's expansionary drive for profits—unique to this mode of production, however environmentally destructive state-socialist regimes may have been—incentivizes capitalists to commandeer nature's gifts, while absolving them of responsibility to replenish and repair. Capital's relation to nature is thus intrinsically extractive, consuming biophysical wealth while disavowing externalities, piling up 'an ever-growing mountain of eco-wreckage: an atmosphere flooded by carbon emissions, climbing temperatures, crumbling polar ice shelves, rising seas clogged with islands of plastic'—'superstorms, mega-droughts, giant locust swarms, jumbo wild fires, titanic flooding; dead zones, poisoned lands, unbreathable air.'[21]

Fraser expands her reading of the historical sequence here to discuss 'socio-ecological regimes of accumulation', examining forms of energetics and modes of expansion—where and how the lines between economy and nature are drawn and what meanings are assigned to each. In the mercantile era, energy sources—wind, water, human and animal muscle power—were essentially continuous with pre-capitalist societies. The rupture lay in the new mode of expansion through expropriation:

---

[20] CC, p. 73.   [21] CC, pp. 76, 81–83.

the conquest of new lands and labour, from the Potosí silver mines to the jute fields of Bengal and the plantations of Sainte-Domingue. The socio-ecology of the liberal-colonial regime was founded on coal and steam, with a new distinction drawn between the booming manufacturing cities and the emptying countryside. Industrialism vaunted the liberation of the forces of production from the constraints of land and labour, yet it rested on the extraction of 'cheap nature' from the periphery. Post-war Keynesian capitalism, seemingly less disreputable in other domains, oversaw a vast expansion in greenhouse-gas emissions through its novel combination of the internal-combustion engine and refined oil, highway construction and suburban living. The present financialized regime 'scrambles energetic geography', as Fraser puts it, but Northern 'post-materialism' still rests on processes of carbon-based mining and manufacturing, from Alaska to the Andes, Mexico to Shenzhen. Indeed, Northern consumption has become increasingly carbon-intensive—air travel, meat eating, concrete buildout—while expropriation has expanded into intellectual-property monopolies over seeds and plants.[22]

Fraser makes her most passionate case here for grasping the different crisis dimensions as an interlinked whole. Environmental questions and social-reproductive ones are closely connected, she argues; both are concerned with matters of life and death. Social reproduction is simultaneously natural and cultural, managing the interface of sociality and biology, community and habitat. Environmentalism is unavoidably political: states choose how to police the boundary between economy and nature, regulating land use, emissions, mining and toxic waste. It is also entangled with the dynamics of expropriation and exploitation. Capitalism is the unifying figure that links them all. 'The political implications are conceptually simple, if practically challenging,' Fraser writes. A viable eco-politics needs to be anti-capitalist and trans-environmental, constructing a planet-wide counter-hegemony that can orient a broad project of transformation, connecting global warming to economic insecurity, the undervaluation of care work, the exorbitant costs of financial and environmental expropriation—and wresting the power to dictate our relation to nature away from a capitalist class primed for expansionary accumulation. The mainstream premise that the environment can be adequately protected without disturbing the structures

[22] CC, pp. 92–102.

of capitalist society is false. A reductive 'ecologism' which sets all else aside to focus on carbon emissions fails to grasp that ecopolitics itself is being fought out in a global context riven by a broader social, economic and political crisis.[23]

Turning, finally, to the question of politics, Fraser acknowledges the force of the diagnosis—by, *inter alia*, Wolfgang Streeck, Colin Crouch, Wendy Brown and Stephen Gill—of a crisis of democracy, in face of oligarchic corporations, supranational regulation and hollowing from within by market ideology. But she proposes a more fundamental contradiction between the imperatives of capital accumulation and the work of the state on which it relies: maintaining a legal framework, sustaining a currency, managing borders and international trade, building infrastructure, mitigating crises. Following Ellen Meiksins Wood, she understands the advent of capitalism as instituting a separation of the political and the economic, with each assigned its own sphere and means of operation; under capitalism, 'the economic is non-political and the political is non-economic'. This meant that large areas of life were beyond democratic political control. The boundary of the economic and the political thus became a site of perpetual contention and potential crisis.[24]

Under mercantile capitalism, the leading absolutist states—first Spain, then France—regulated commerce internally, but profited from external plunder and long-distance trade within an expanding world market; this international 'value logic' eventually fostered the urban merchant-capitalist strata which would rise against the *ancien régime*. Under liberal-colonial *laissez-faire*, a modernized political order instead limited itself to guaranteeing the conditions required for unfettered capital accumulation: property rights, stable currency and suppression of revolts at home; a strong navy and expansionist military-imperial policy abroad. Roiled by financial crashes, wars and slumps, laissez faire gave way to a greater role for state intervention under the mid-century Keynesian regime. From the 1980s, this was in turn supplanted by the neoliberal financialized regime, with state policy increasingly at the mercy of the market. The present era is increasingly one of 'governance without government'; transnational regulations pre-empt social reform and impose

---

[23] CC, 87–89, 105, 77, 85, 110, 77.
[24] CC, pp. 116, 119, 121–2. Ellen Meiksins Wood's classic statement is 'The Separation of the Economic and the Political in Capitalism', NLR 127, May–June 1981.

finance capital's agenda—most dramatically in the rule of the Troika (IMF, ECB, EC) over Greece in 2015.[25]

This 'democratic deficit', Fraser argues, is the historically specific form that capitalism's inherent political contradiction assumes under the current regime of accumulation, which has so diminished democratic power that it cannot solve the urgent problems it confronts: the climate crisis, economic insecurity, the breakdown of social care. It thus becomes an integral part of the general crisis—and cannot be resolved without transforming the societal order, root and branch. This political dysfunction found a subjective correlate in 2016, as tens of millions of voters defected from 'politics as usual'. Victories for Brexit and Trump were rebukes to the architects of neoliberalism, Fraser writes. The fortunes of the populists have waxed and waned, often due to their disappointing spells in office, but 2016 signalled a shift in the political winds: the scope for public intervention broadened, the veil of neoliberal common sense was torn, the boundary between the political and the economic began to shift; yet capital still retains its grip on the levers of power. Politically, we face uncertain terrain, with no broadly legitimate hegemonic bloc, nor any credible counter-hegemonic challenger. The system's impasses will continue to mount until one can be assembled.[26]

Sketching a possible response to the crisis, Fraser thinks not in terms of a new regime of capital accumulation, but a new conception of socialism. If such a possibility seems far off, *Cannibal Capitalism* insists that it is still worth discussing the real emergent possibilities—'the potentials for human freedom, well-being and happiness'—that capitalism has brought within reach but cannot actualize. Such a conception would need to re-think the socialized economy's relation to its background conditions, 'to reimagine their interrelations', reversing the current priorities: not growth for the sake of private accumulation but the

---

[25] CC, pp. 124–30.

[26] CC, pp. 130–33. Earlier versions published first as 'Legitimation Crisis? On the Political Contradictions of Financialized Capitalism', *Critical Historical Studies*, vol. 2, no. 2, 2015 and in *Was stimmt nicht mit der Demokratie? Eine Debatte mit Klaus Dörre, Nancy Fraser, Stephan Lessenich und Hartmut Rosa*, ed. Hanna Ketterer and Karina Becker, Berlin 2019. See also Nancy Fraser, *The Old is Dying and the New Cannot Be Born: From Progressive Neoliberalism to Trump and Beyond*, London and New York 2019. A version of the main essay was originally published as 'From Progressive Neoliberalism to Trump and Beyond', *American Affairs*, vol. 1, no.4, Winter 2017.

nurturing of people, safe-guarding of nature and democratic self-rule. It would make the growth question a political one, offering a rule of thumb for markets under socialism: no markets 'at the bottom'—basic needs (food, shelter, clothing, healthcare, clean water, etc) would be subject to democratic discussion, but provided as a right—and no markets 'at the top', for the surplus would be seen as the collective wealth of society as a whole, and allocated by a collective planning process. In between, there could be space for experimentation, a mix of possibilities: commons, co-operatives, self-organizing associations—rendering the boundaries between background conditions more porous and more responsive.[27]

Questions

The richness and originality of Fraser's construction speaks for itself. It's hard to think of a single contemporary writer who has attempted a conceptual synthesis on this scale and of this complexity—a model resolutely radical in intent. Attempts to enlarge our understanding of capitalism have generally examined it in relation to one extra domain at a time. There is a rich literature on imperialism, slavery and racialization, examining the American experience in particular——and an impressive body of work on social reproduction.[28] Eco-Marxists such as James O'Connor, John Bellamy Foster, Mike Davis, Andreas Malm and Jason Moore have produced powerful analyses historicizing the relation of capitalism to the environment. Many thinkers have tried to probe the connections between economic and political malaise in recent years, among them Peter Mair, Colin Crouch, Wendy Brown and John Judis, with Wolfgang Streeck's *Buying Time* a standout explanation.[29] But Fraser's is surely the first attempt to date to map all these dimensions as an interrelated and determinate whole—and not just for the neoliberal era or the advanced-capitalist North, but on a world scale and across a span of centuries.

---

[27] CC, pp. 151–57.

[28] On imperialism, racialization and slavery, the tradition descends from DuBois, Oliver Cromwell Cox and Eric Williams to Orlando Pattison, Robin Blackburn, Manning Marable, Barbara Fields, Cedric Johnson, Barbara Ransby and Keeanga-Yamahtta Taylor, among others. On social reproduction, the line descending from—and complicating—Engels would include Maria Mies, Lisa Vogel, Wally Seccombe, Johanna Brenner, Jacqueline Jones, Tithi Bhattacharya, Gabriel Winant and Arlie Hochschild.

[29] Wolfgang Streeck, *Buying Time: The Delayed Crisis of Democratic Capitalism*, London and New York 2014.

Designedly schematic, Fraser's model provides a valuable heuristic for empirical testing and conceptual investigation. Thematically, the connections with her earlier thinking will be apparent. As in 'From Redistribution to Recognition?', she argues for a transformative politics, tackling deep structures, against the affirmative ameliorations of neo-liberal progressivism; the 21st century has vindicated her insistence on capitalist inequity, so out of fashion in the 1990s. Methodologically, too, there are many continuities—above all, in the patterning of social relations by boldly abstract categories, augmented by occasional deep dives into empirical exemplum, usually cultural in form (it is very rare to find facts and figures in her writing, which operates in the realm of social theory, not social science). Fraser's writing has always prized clarity and accessibility, but the style here is avowedly more popular (sometimes at a cost: chapter titles punning on the 'cannibal' metaphor). Conceptually, a selection of Marxian categories have come to the fore—production and reproduction, expropriation and exploitation, core and periphery—and Rawlsian 'justice' is now more of a social metric than an endpoint. The categories here are also distinctively spatial, in a manner reminiscent of Habermas—foreground and backgrounds, shifts in perspective, a 'topography' of capitalist society—but also discursive, in more deconstructionist spirit: a front story and back story, each abode governed by a unique ontological 'grammar'.

It is not always easy to know how to fill in or re-people these abstract categories with living realities—to assess their accuracy as conceptual tools, or judge their usefulness as guides to action, in the light of other knowledge. In interviews, Fraser has clarified that she sees the root of the general crisis in the drive for profits of a small group of powerful actors—Wall Street, Big Oil, Big Pharma, Silicon Valley; Walmart, GE, Cargill and the like—ravaging the 'non-economic' realms.[30] An empirical road-test might ask how far her model serves to illuminate contemporary struggles. If we take, for example, the conflict over resource extraction in Ecuador, Fraser's heuristic would compel us to take into account not only the operations of the giant Northern mining companies and the habitats of the local communities, but also the politics of the Quito government, the strength of the Ecuadorian fiscal state and the social-reproductive implications for both the indigenous groups involved and the wider population, in the context of a broader conjunctural crisis.

---

[30] See for example, Rhoda Feng, 'Nancy Fraser's Lessons from the Long History of Capitalism', *The Nation*, 29 November 2022.

Or take the overlapping domains revealed by the long struggle of the Gilets Jaunes against Macron's petrol tax: a 'progressive neoliberal' environmental measure rejected on economic and social-reproductive (*fin du mois*) grounds by struggling formal-sector workers, their protests brutally suppressed by the state, in an EU that is sucking democratic decision-making into an unaccountable void.

The notion of boundary struggles helps to open up a wider understanding of recent battles in the US. Abortion rights, for example, pit women's reproductive autonomy against political and juridical opponents—not just the conservative Supreme Court but the Democratic congressional majorities that have refused to legislate for women's control over their own bodies. Or take Black Lives Matter: through Fraser's heuristic, not only a resistance movement against racialized state violence, but an expression of the harm caused by material inequality in an America struggling at once to re-gear and to decarbonize its financialized, de-industrialized economy against overseas rivals.

On a preliminary test, then, Fraser's construction seems genuinely useful. Does it also serve as a dynamic explanatory model for capitalist society, proposing laws of motion and theories of causality as, say, the concept of the mode of production aspired to do? This raises a conceptual question: the nature of the 'background zones', and their relations to the economic 'foreground' and to each other. It is an issue explored at length in Fraser's illuminating dialogue with Rahel Jaeggi, *Capitalism: A Conversation in Critical Theory*, which forms an intriguing critical-theoretical pendant to *Cannibal Capitalism*. Here, Jaeggi poses a series of probing questions. Are the background zones 'inside' the capitalist system, *à la* Lukács, or outside it, *à la* Polanyi? What are the relations between foreground and backgrounds—determinism, functional necessity, dependencies in several directions? What changes the dynamics within each field and the equilibria between them? Fraser explains that she sees the backgrounds on which the capitalist economy depends as non- or, perhaps, semi-commodified, by analogy with Wallerstein's concept of semi-proletarianized households, which derive a good part of their subsistence from non-wage sources, including state transfers, informal reciprocity and self-provisioning. There is an objective structural argument here, she argues, invoked by Hegel in the *Philosophy of Right*—where the sphere of contractual relations is possible only on the basis of background non-contractual social relations—as well as by

Polanyi in *The Great Transformation*, where markets depend for their existence on non-marketized society.

Yet isn't Fraser's division between 'capitalist economy' and 'non-economic zones' haunted by the ghost of Habermas's 'economic system' versus pristine 'lifeworld'? Jaeggi presses her on this question. Is Fraser repeating the same move that she once criticized in Habermas, seeing the economy preying on these 'innocent' domains?[31] Fraser denies this. She doesn't see the economy 'colonizing' these zones, in Habermas's terms, but rather a process of contestation, as capital attempts to 'devour' them. The resulting configuration is the outcome of struggle, based on the balance of social forces. While non-commodified and outside the *economy*, the zones are inside capitalist society as a whole. To see social reproduction or nature as 'outside' capitalist society and inherently opposed to it would be a romantic view, she argues—imagining that they could be sites for counter-hegemony, when they are in fact symbiotic with capital. At the same time, they are sites of internal contradiction for capitalism, generating their own non-economic values—for social reproduction, ideals of love and solidarity; for nature, ecological values of planetary stewardship; for politics, principles of democracy and self-determination. Fraser's both-and form of argumentation—so illuminating when applied to the problem of mediating between economic and cultural claims for justice—begins to confound when deployed to insist on the irrevocable entanglement of the economic and its non-economic others.

In any case, is it not worse to be 'devoured' than to be colonized? This raises the further question of how seriously Fraser's 'cannibal' metaphor should be taken. Her initial note on this is playful, suggesting that the term's different meanings offer various avenues for analysis.[32] Its origin lies in a corruption of the Spanish term for the natives of the Caribbean, alleged by the conquistadors to be eaters of human flesh. As a verb, it may also refer to dismemberment—dismantling the component parts of a machine in order to put them to use them for something else; in biology, analogously, autophagy is the recycling of parts of cells. In astronomy, 'cannibalization' indicates a body that exerts a gravitational pull on another, incorporating its mass. And finally, there is the ouroboros, the mythical serpent or dragon that eats its own tail—an Ancient Egyptian symbol of eternal renewal, through the cycle of life, death and rebirth. In

---

[31] C:ACCT, p. 51.   [32] CC, pp. xiii–xiv.

Cannibal Capitalism, it is not always clear which meaning we should have mind. Is capitalism an ouroboros—the Lukácsian, internalist view—devouring its own body? Or is it a cannibal—the Polanyian, externalist one—consuming its like (the extra-economic) but not its very self?

The distinction may seem pedantic, but followed to its logical conclusion it has ramifications for Fraser's assessment of capitalism's tendency towards crisis and its capacity to survive. Put bluntly: a cannibal, if voracious enough, may one day run out of food; the symbolic serpent will not. Certainly, an account like Fraser's or Wallerstein's that locates capitalism's origins in sixteenth-century Spain is more likely to depict it as a form subject to continual self-renewal than one that begins with the growth of industrial capitalism in Britain in the early 1800s or its generalization across the advanced powers in the 1870s, with a third of the world under avowedly communist regimes for a good part of the twentieth century. The analysis of the changing regimes of accumulation from the 1500s onwards, at once Schumpeterian in its focus on the creative destruction powering the system and Kuhnian in its use of paradigm shifts, reveals an underlying functionalist logic: capitalism is because capitalism does. A new structure—for example, the two-wage household—emerges as the old one enters crisis and acts to restore homeostasis to the system; an explanatory model which, as Arthur Stinchcombe demonstrated in *Constructing Social Theories*, tends to see a conservative tendency in the existing social order.[33] The desire to counter this may lead to an added emphasis on self-inflicted catastrophe as a way to break the chain.

The cannibal metaphor is perhaps best read as a rhetorical device, a flash of hyperbole for consciousness-raising purposes. Fraser's non-metaphorical formulation—that capital's drive for endless accumulation threatens to 'destabilize' or 'imperil' its conditions of possibility—is more compelling. Yet this raises the question of the commensurability of the 'background zones'. Destabilization seems an entirely plausible fate—or actuality—for the environment. Concretizing analysis might identify geophysical limits to capitalist growth in the form of climate destabilization, resource exhaustion or a social-system collapse outpacing green capital's ability to achieve any real impact.[34] Fraser hints

---

[33] Arthur Stinchcombe, *Constructing Social Theories*, Cambridge, MA 1960, pp. 80–101.
[34] See Thomas Meaney, 'Fortunes of the Green New Deal', NLR 138, Nov–Dec 2022.

at such a conclusion, giving her programme the provisional title of 'ecosocialism', but holds back from elevating the ecological to the role of primary political concern. It remains an equal among other abodes. Yet it is hard to see the crisis of care posing quite the same existential threat as global warming. This is not to deny the tragic social fallout that has followed the twentieth-century's historic working-class defeats, of which Middle America's opioid epidemic and deaths of despair are emblematic. Not only for feminist reasons but morally, too, Fraser has good reason to foreground the strains placed on social reproduction. But with China's entry into the world market, global capital has benefited from a glut of cheap labour; young workers from Central America and elsewhere are banging on America's doors. In an instrumental sense, capital has no need to fret about labour's perpetuation.

The position of the political as a background zone is based on Meiksins Wood's theorization of its separation from the economic—but this can be misleading. It is true that economic compulsion in a cash economy supplies the whip for labour. But within the ruling bloc, wealth and power are joined by a dense connective tissue of professional, social, institutional, educational and familial bonds. Here the historical view might have an advantage over philosophical analysis, pointing to the role of the ruling class. Fraser puts this nicely when she speaks of the hollow Wizard of Oz quality of today's politicians, who strut and preen before a curtain that conceals the real powers. Her judgements on Trump, Biden and the rest are admirably sober.[35] Yet it would be useful to have a fuller sense of political power—the vast institutional complex of the state, its immense powers of coercion and surveillance, its tireless machinery of ideological self-justification—to complement the analysis of the multinationals and the banks.

Politics in *Cannibal Capitalism* is mainly treated in terms of democracy, or as non-agonistic public authority. But public authority is only non-agonistic when it is entirely sure of its command. Fraser argues persuasively that the solution to a crisis in one background realm must simultaneously address those in the others; a total critique yields a total programme of action. But where to start? Calls to change everything, to listen to everyone, to acknowledge that everything is capitalism, can be alternately inspiring or demotivating. New kinds of transitional strategy will need to be elaborated to get us from here to there and they will

---

[35] CC, pp. 135–36.

require an understanding of state power to inform them, as also of elite dissensus.[36] Fraser is surely right to stress that connections must be made across the boundaries; but decisions about action require a principle of priority, a model of politically targeted alliances.

None of this is to detract from the immense achievement of Fraser's synthesis. Her lucid re-politicization of critical theory constitutes a real advance for radical thought. For her, the work of social philosophy involves conceiving the living links between *Kapitalkritik* and anti-capitalist action. For decades, Fraser has defied intellectual trends in defence of a truly socialist feminism, often provoking scrutiny and critique, as we have seen, from theorist colleagues. Poststructuralist linguistic feminism was at its high-tide when she first asserted the importance of an emancipatory political philosophy that paid attention to redistribution—and to the material impacts of Clinton-era social policy on the marginalized—as well as to recognition. Later, at the peak of neoliberal feminism, she sought to defend the project of the second wave from its 'uncanny double', represented in the corporate-friendly forms of diversity and inclusion for a privileged minority of women, at the expense of the rest. Instead of focusing solely on the single issue of gendered experience, she has pursued a research agenda so wide, ambitious and rigorous as to arrive at a unique description of the entire capitalist system, historic and contemporary. Current left intellectual life owes an incalculable debt to her for keeping such questions alive during periods in which they were overlooked or dismissed in political and academic life alike—as well as for revivifying the debate at a time when the critical mapping of capitalism's complexities is a task as urgent as it is daunting.

---

[36] Richard Lachmann, *First Class Passengers on a Sinking Ship: Elite Politics and the Decline of Great Powers*, London and New York 2020. Lachmann's research reveals a bricolage of compromises and fixes, under constant repair, to balance competing interests.

Leuven University Press

www.lup.be - info@lup.be

Francis Alÿs. The Nature of the Game

Gerard-Jan Claes, Stéphane Symons (eds)

€ 30,00 / £29.00 | PB
ISBN 9789462703841
Open Access ebook

Watching, Waiting The Photographic Representation of Empty Places

Sandra Križić Roban, Ana Šverko (eds)

€ 59,50 / £54.00 | PB
ISBN 9789462703759
Open Access ebook

Dirk Lauwaert Selected Writings, 1983-2008

Herman Asselberghs, Robbrecht Desmet, Bart Meuleman, Peter Jan Perquy (eds)

€ 35,00 / £34.00 | PB
ISBN 9789462703858
ebook

The Belgian Photonovel, 1954-1985 An Introduction

Clarissa Colangelo

€ 45,00 / £42.00 | PB
ISBN 9789462703704
Open Access ebook

HOW TO ORDER

Sales representation and Order fulfilment UK: Ingram Publisher Services UK – www.ingrampublisherservices.co.uk
IPSUK.Cservs@ingramcontent.com. Sales representation USA: Cornell University Press - www.cornellpress.cornell.edu -
Order fulfilment USA: Longleaf Services, Inc. - customerservice@longleafservices.org

 ORDER ONLINE AT WWW.LUP.BE

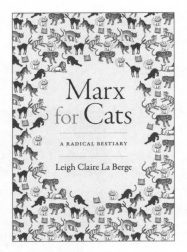

ALYSSA BATTISTONI & GEOFF MANN

CLIMATE BIDENOMICS

OW SHOULD Bidenomics be assessed so far? In their 'Seven Theses on American Politics', Dylan Riley and Robert Brenner argue that the long slowdown in growth rates has led to the emergence of a new regime of accumulation in the US, 'political capitalism', defined by 'politically engineered upward redistribution'—so much so that 'raw political power, rather than productive investment, is the key determinant of the rate of return'. This, Riley and Brenner argue, has transformed America's electoral landscape and recomposed the two party coalitions, producing 'a vicious, narrowly divided politics of zero-sum redistribution, largely axed on conflicts of material interest *within* the working class', between groups defined by education level and race.[1] In the debate that has followed, contributions have spun out in a range of directions: the role of class and its relation to 'material interest' in the US; the dynamics driving party–class dealignment—workers abandoning the Democrats to vote Republican, high earners moving in the opposite direction—and prospects for countering it; the geopolitics of what Lola Seaton calls the Biden Administration's 'green-nationalist industrialization drive'; the reliability of Brenner's manufacturing-centric 'long downturn' account of 'secular stagnation'; and in general, the outlook for left politics today, class-based or not.[2]

What has been surprisingly absent from the discussion, given the centrality of 'green industrial policy' to Biden's agenda—not to mention the wider state of the planet, with this summer the hottest ever recorded—is climate change. Of course, the pieces gesture to the role of the energy transition in the White House's domestic and geopolitical manoeuvring, and note the Administration's decarbonization pledges, if only to point out their inadequacy. But climate change itself goes virtually unaddressed as a specific problem with political and economic significance in its own right. In this respect, the discussion in these pages mirrors the broader state of political debate. The Inflation Reduction Act, perhaps the flagship policy of Bidenomics, was hailed as a bill that might 'save civilization' when it was passed in August 2022.[3] Since then, it has been almost entirely assimilated to the more general 'Bidenomics' frame: once discussed in relation to the Green New Deal, it is now more often evaluated alongside the bipartisan Infrastructure Investment and Jobs Act and the CHIPS and Science Act, and assessed in terms of domestic investment and geopolitical dynamics rather than decarbonization targets or climate impacts.

The political issues upon which the discussion in NLR has focused, in turn, are not 'about' the climate in any real sense. Perhaps commentators have taken the Administration's claims about the IRA's climate *bona fides* at face value—or assume that mentions of 'green tech' suffice as climate analysis. But climate change demands explicit and focused attention. Two broad questions structure our reflections on this front: first, what Bidenomics means for the climate; and second, what climate change means for Bidenomics, and for politics more generally. But before turning to these, it is worth taking a more granular look at the political conditions and the domestic and geopolitical dynamics that shaped the IRA, analysing both its objectives and its contradictions as a political strategy. Why did the IRA take the form it did, and what does it tell us about the 'political capitalism' diagnosis?

Inside the IRA?

If the Inflation Reduction Act has a claim to be the most significant Federal climate legislation in US history, this is largely because it is the first such bill ever enacted. While its provisions are clearly inadequate to the scale of the climate crisis, the IRA's defenders have argued that it is at least a start on which to build. If eco-socialists continue to engage with the formal policy process, both through the outside pressures of

[1] Dylan Riley and Robert Brenner, 'Seven Theses on American Politics', NLR 138, Nov–Dec 2022.
[2] Matthew Karp, 'Party and Class in American Politics', NLR 139, Jan–Feb 2023; Tim Barker, 'Some Questions about Political Capitalism', NLR 140/141, Mar–June 2023; Aaron Benanav, 'A Dissipating Glut?', NLR 140/141, Mar–June 2023; Lola Seaton, 'Reflections on Political Capitalism', NLR 142, July–Aug 2023. See also Grey Anderson, 'Strategies of Denial', NLR–*Sidecar*, 15 June 2023.
[3] Paul Krugman, 'Did Democrats Just Save Civilization?', *New York Times*, 8 August 2022.

activism and the inside work of congressional politics, climate policy will get closer to the scale and scope required. The hope is that the bundle of subsidies, tax breaks, infrastructure investment and market protectionism will unite green-tech boosters with big capital, organized labour and the beneficiaries of the growth-to-come. If this coalition-building is successful, more green-industrial policy will ensue, until new clean industries are the self-sustaining powerhouses of a thriving economy.

We return to the issue of green growth below. But the issues raised in the 'Seven Theses' debate thus far point towards a different question: why did Biden do anything about climate at all? Riley and Brenner diagnose Bidenism as an appeal to the material interests of the Democrats' new core constituency, the college-educated, with its high valuation of 'expertise' and of 'credentialled labour power'. The IRA might at first seem easily assimilable to this project—catnip for the 'science is real' brigade. Certainly, a key element of Biden's embrace of climate politics can be understood in terms of intra-Democratic Party factional struggles. He was elected amid a surge of climate activism both within the US and worldwide: the 2020 election was perhaps the first in which climate change was a serious topic of discussion, driven largely by pressure from the left wing of the party. After a bitterly fought primary season, when the Democratic establishment closed ranks against Sanders and handed Biden the nomination, climate change proved a crucial issue around which to forge a truce, exemplified by the Sanders–Biden Unity Task Force on the climate crisis. The Biden Administration then put forward the surprisingly ambitious Build Back Better plan, which proposed to pair major investments in decarbonization and care—including support for families with children, an expansion of paid leave, and funding for childhood education. That ambition, of course, was sharply tempered by subsequent negotiations in Congress; for months it seemed that a Federal climate package would once again be scuttled on the shoals of America's partisan divide. Yet the climate provisions survived, if in the enfeebled form of the IRA. Why did they squeak through, while proposed investments in 'care infrastructure' and other social welfare programmes were abandoned?

Riley and Brenner's account of 'political capitalism', in which the Republicans and the Democrats deliver material benefits to their bases—the less educated and the highly credentialled, respectively—fails to provide a convincing answer. The Democratic base, after all, contains large numbers of health care workers and dual-income households, who would presumably prefer major investments in care. Silicon Valley threw its weight behind the legislation; eventually so too did automakers and—more surprisingly—fossil fuel companies themselves. But the IRA is not so much a sop to a powerful green-capital lobby as an effort to create a new fraction of green capital—if not quite from scratch, then from the scraps of the Obama-era stimulus package, which helped catalyse America's solar industry. Certainly, the Democratic leadership now takes climate change more seriously; but as Gore can testify, elite Democratic concerns about global warming have taken a back seat to other issues for decades.

The centrality of climate investments to Bidenomics is better understood as an effort to thread the tricky political needle debated in these pages. Riley and Brenner argue that politics in the present have abandoned 'even the *hope* of growth', hence their glossing of Bidenomics as 'deficit spending without growth'. But the IRA is clearly an attempt to assemble a new growth programme around a novel political coalition, as Ted Fertik and Tim Sahay have argued.[4] The hope of restoring growth through a classic strategy of (re)industrialization delivering widely distributed economic wealth—as opposed to distributing social benefits directly via spending on low-growth sectors like care—plainly animates it.

Rather than funnelling zero-sum benefits to the Democratic Party's highly educated base, the IRA is in part a strategic attempt to reach precisely the set of working-class voters who have been abandoning it. The legislation itself was ultimately the result of a closed-door deal between Senators Joe Manchin and Chuck Schumer, and its shape reflects the Democratic Party dilemma—a negotiation between West Virginia and New York. Many commentators have reasonably emphasized Manchin's ties to the coal industry as the central force motivating his initial recalcitrance, and the IRA's eventual concessions to the fossil industry. Equally relevant to the character of the legislation, however, is Manchin's position as the closest thing to a 'red state' senator in the Democratic Party, and Schumer's especial vulnerability to the left in his home state. Manchin and Schumer, in other words, represent the elements of an increasingly fragile historic coalition, and their attempt to forge a new compromise

---

[4] Ted Fertik and Tim Sahay, 'Bidenomics and Climate Action: The Case of the Inflation Reduction Act', talk at Brown University, 3 February 2023, available on YouTube.

that can carry the Party into the future also channels many of the pressures that are presently fraying it.

This becomes clear when we look more closely at the IRA's provisions. The law subsidizes green technology on both sides: production and consumption; supply and demand. The demand side is primarily a boon to Democratic voters with disposable income and commitments to green consumption. EV tax credits are most likely to be used by the better-off middle class, while ecologically conscious homeowners can increase asset values installing heat pumps, solar panels and charging stations in the garage. Investments on the supply side, however, are effectively the opposite of delivering for one's base: an estimated 80 per cent of private clean tech and semiconductor investments announced thus far have been in Republican districts.[5] For all the Biden Administration's embrace of workers and organized labour, the IRA's political strategy assumes that private capital will flow most generously to the places where unionization is most difficult, and eventually into the pockets of red-state voters disinclined to support climate policy, let alone a Green New Deal, who might nevertheless welcome the jobs created in Sunbelt solar installations, Texas wind farms and 'green tech' manufacturing concentrated in Southern right-to-work states. This strategy might help produce a durable bipartisan coalition for green investment that can survive party polarization. But it is a risky political strategy for a party hoping to renew its legitimacy, particularly in the face of front-page economic headwinds like inflation. Even if Bidenomics creates green jobs, will it get any credit for them from the voters it needs most?

The likelihood that green jobs will not be union jobs, moreover, is not lost on the unions themselves. Equally troubling is the fact that EV manufacturing requires considerably fewer workers than making cars powered by internal-combustion engines. Worry that the EV boom threatens labour in the car industry has led the United Auto Workers to put the conditions of the green transition at the heart of their historic contract fight, in which they are seeking to bring all EV and battery workers under the UAW's 'master agreement' with the big three American carmakers, GM, Ford and Chrysler/Stellantis.[6] Although headlines duly

---

[5] Amanda Chu, Oliver Roeder, Myles McCormick, 'Republican Districts Dominate US Clean Technology Investment Boom', *FT*, 13 August 2023.
[6] Keith Brower Brown, 'As Big 3 Auto Contracts Expire: Hurried Line Speeds and Horrible Hours, *Labor Notes*, 25 July 2023.

note 'tensions' between labour and climate goals, in fact it marks the most unequivocal support for a green transition from the segments of the American labour movement most directly affected by the prospect, and the strongest step yet towards the realization of the much-discussed 'just transition'. Citing frustration with the Administration's half-hearted support, the UAW has thus far declined to endorse Biden's re-election campaign—a savvy move that has pressured the Administration to deliver new subsidies for union EV plants, and driven Biden himself to visit a UAW picket line.[7]

The UAW strike, which began on 15 September with initial walk-outs at three assembly factories—a GM plant in Wentzville, Missouri, a Ford plant in Wayne, Michigan, and a Jeep plant run by Stellantis in Toledo, Ohio—reveals many of the contradictory elements brought into play by Bidenomics: an increasingly active labour movement, energized by a tight jobs market, confronting a supposedly labour-friendly president; a once-mighty union simultaneously emboldened and threatened by the promise of state-subsidized reindustrialization; the hope for a new class compromise in an industry whose growth model assumes access to non-unionized labour; and the prospect that the workforce of an industry intensely associated with carbon emissions might help lead the way to a greener future. As Gabriel Winant has noted, moreover, the rise of the UAW's more militant president, Shawn Fain, is the product of a new class coalition between the highly educated, downwardly mobile workers recently organized by the UAW and reform elements within its traditional membership.[8]

Yet the auto-workers' strike also showcases the political fragility of the Bidenomics strategy for a green transition. Although Biden repeats the mantra, 'When I hear climate, I think jobs', he sometimes seems to hope that no one will hear mention of the climate at all. Green subsidies will supposedly be better received if they are not discussed in terms of global warming. But the right is hardly inclined to keep the secret. The rebound

---

[7] Workers at Ford's gigantic industrial complex under construction in Stanton, Tennessee will not automatically be required to join the UAW, leading the union's president, Shawn Fain, to criticize the Biden Administration for signing off on loans to the car-maker (the investment is worth $5.6bn), without agreeing wage requirements in advance: 'Will the Auto Workers' Strike Jeopardize Joe Biden's Manufacturing Boom?', *Economist*, 24 September 2023.

[8] Gabriel Winant, 'Eight and Skate', NYRB, 23 September 2023.

of the US oil and gas industry following sanctions on Russian hydrocarbons has made it hard for Trump to accuse Biden of waging a war on oil, as he accused Obama of destroying coal. Trump has instead seized the opportunity to attack Biden on electric vehicles: 'This ridiculous Green New Deal crusade is causing car prices to skyrocket while setting the stage for the destruction of American auto production.' Manchin has joined in, attacking a loophole granting foreign automakers access to some EV subsidies as 'illegal' and contrary to the intent of the legislation he himself shaped.[9] In fact, although EVs are, on average, more expensive than cars with internal-combustion engines, the recent surge in car prices has little to do with any green transition. It is, rather, the predictable result of supply-chain disruption, ballooning vehicle sizes and automakers' decisions to prioritize higher-margin models. It is notable, moreover, that these would-be populists have thrown in with consumers faced with sticker shock rather than workers seeking to increase stagnant wages. It was Manchin who blocked a tax credit for union-made EVs, while Trump recently inveighed against EVs at a non-union autoparts manufacturer in Michigan.[10]

The facts, however, are clearly beside the point. Electric vehicles offer a convenient issue for a demagoguery pitched at the growing partisan split along urban-rural lines—an important political division in the US, largely unaddressed in the 'Seven Theses' debate. Most Americans are dependent on cars, especially the suburban voters so vigorously courted by both parties. The spectre of a full-blown climate culture war, previewed in warnings that the Green New Deal would deprive Americans of their hamburgers and pickup trucks, is surely part of the reason why the Biden Administration has opted for a one-to-one replacement of internal combustion engines by electric vehicles, rather than the investment in clean public transit or densification proposed by Green New Deal advocates. If Trump misrepresents the causes of high vehicle prices (among much else), he is not wrong to note that most EVs are too expensive for most people, even with tax credits—credits that don't, at least at present, apply to cheaper models whose components don't meet IRA standards, like the Nissan Leaf. Inflation, moreover, makes high prices

---

[9] Jonathan Weisman, 'Trump Seeks UAW's Support as the Union Wavers on Backing Biden', NYT, 20 July 2023; Josh Siegel, 'Manchin's "Playing with Fire"—and Some Democrats Are Tired of the Drama', *Politico*, 1 May 2023.
[10] Alex Press, 'Trump Is Speaking Tonight in Michigan at a Nonunion Auto Shop, as a Guest of Its Boss', *Jacobin*, 27 September 2023.

an easy political target. If Bidenomics is a bet that state support for green capital can revive growth and reconsolidate Democratic Party power, it remains a risky gamble.

Geopolitical logics

Riskier still is the Administration's move to attach climate policy to its geopolitical strategy. When Biden hears 'climate', we might say, he not only thinks 'jobs'; he thinks 'China'. As Grey Anderson has argued on *Sidecar*, the Administration's green industrial drive is a key element in its pursuit of supply-chain security and renewed American hegemony. For Anderson, it is this 'geostrategic rationale' that powers the national-investment drive: 'Viewed from the halls of power, the anti-China orientation of US industrial policy is not an unfortunate by-product of the green "transition", but its motivating purpose.'[11] While Trump drastically escalated anti-China rhetoric, aspects of some such programme have nonetheless been long in development. In 2007, Thomas Friedman pitched the Green New Deal as 'geostrategic, geoeconomic, capitalistic and patriotic', a way for America 'to get its groove back': 'We will need to find a way to reknit America at home, reconnect America abroad and restore America to its natural place in the global order—as the beacon of progress, hope and inspiration. I have an idea how. It's called "green"'.[12] A few years later, gearing up for his 'pivot to Asia', Obama pledged to 'win the future': 'to out-innovate, out-educate, and out-build the rest of the world', through, among other things, investments in clean energy.[13]

Under Biden, of course, China is explicitly and directly targeted as the US's major competitor. Anderson is right to point to the dangers of this development. Yet he conflates too much in his suggestion that there is a 'relational logic between expanded domestic spending and an increasingly aggressive Pacific policy'. Anderson is critical of the 'eco-socialist left' for being slow to criticize the Administration's hawkish turn, suggesting its climate objectives may have clouded its judgement. '"Environmental justice" or atomic showdown over the Taiwan Strait?', he asks. 'Critical assessments of Bidenomics ought to be sure which is

---

[11] Anderson, 'Strategies of Denial'.
[12] Thomas Friedman, 'The Power of Green', *New York Times Magazine*, 15 April 2007.
[13] 'Remarks by the President in State of the Union Address', 25 January 2011; available at obamawhitehouse.archives.gov

which.' But it is not the IRA but the bipartisan CHIPS Act that has been at the centre of feints over Taiwan; the export controls that have been described as an 'act of economic war' explicitly target semiconductor exports.[14] These policies seek to obstruct access to advanced semiconductor technology for China specifically, and to strangle the development of industrial capacity that requires it, particularly for anything with potential military application.

The IRA's 'Buy American' provisions undoubtedly exacerbate any incipient 'New Cold War'. It is obvious that the US hopes to become economically competitive with China on green tech; but as discussed below, the IRA's subsidies and 'local content requirements' have come as more of a shock to Europe than to Beijing. EV production does require semiconductors, but the IRA does not seek to block China from manufacturing EVs or solar photovoltaics (PV) outright, nor from selling them to the rest of the world. Not that it could if it tried: unlike sophisticated semiconductors, the global production of these technologies is already dominated by the PRC. Chinese EV manufacturers currently lead the world in sales, though very few of the buyers are American—not least because of tariffs on Chinese cars imposed by the Trump Administration and renewed by Biden.[15] US-based manufacturers will be hard-pressed to catch up; they are unlikely to compete with Chinese producers on either price or quality, especially in emerging markets like India and Brazil. China is so dominant in solar PV technology, meanwhile, that the US can't set up major trade barriers to these technologies without derailing its own decarbonization goals.[16] At present, China produces 84 per cent of the world's polysilicon, a key material in solar panels, and almost four-fifths of the low-purity gallium critical to battery manufacture (Beijing imposed an export ban on the metal in retaliation for the CHIPS Act).[17]

It is simply not possible to decarbonize quickly without Chinese technology. Indeed, the fastest way for the US to switch to renewable energy

[14] Alex Palmer, '"An Act of War": Inside America's Silicon Blockade against China', *NYT Magazine*, 12 July 2023.
[15] David Ferris and Joshua Posaner, 'Miles Apart: The US and Europe Diverge on China Car Threat', *Politico*, 23 June 2023.
[16] 'Solar PV Global Supply Chains', IEA Special Report, July 2022.
[17] Matt Blois, 'The US Solar Industry Has a Supply Problem', *Chemical & Engineering News*, 18 September 2022; US Geological Survey, 'Mineral Commodity Summaries', January 2022.

would be through massive public spending on the installation of clean-tech purchased from China—a strategy that would be yet another blow to American manufacturing labour, though likely amenable to the politically powerful building trades. Recognizing these limits, in 2022, Biden announced a two-year pause on extending Obama-era tariffs against Chinese solar imports, bowing to domestic solar-panel installers who said that the transition to renewables would stall if the Administration went ahead with them. Chinese factories based in the US, such as JA Solar in Arizona, are making large-scale investments—in this case, creating 600 local jobs—thanks to the IRA. In May 2023, the Treasury clarified that projects using photovoltaic cells manufactured in the PRC would be eligible for IRA tax credits.[18] In these instances, *pace* Anderson, domestic climate goals would appear to be having a cooling effect on the escalating trade war—though it is hard to know how much when climate policy must so often travel incognito.

The response from American solar-manufacturing companies, meanwhile, highlights a potentially significant split within green capital—one we might expect to become increasingly visible across other subsectors. Solar installers, in need of China's low-cost panels, have cheered the decision to roll back tariffs, while solar manufacturers are up in arms.[19] The Biden Administration is backing protectionist barriers against the import of affordable Chinese EVs, but it is not hard to imagine other industries, from electrification infrastructure to appliance manufacture, running up against their own internal divisions over the costs and benefits of cheap China-made inputs—and against the interests of nascent labour movements in these sectors.

The key point is that while the IRA reflects a new alignment of economic and security policy, it is not in itself a particularly serious threat to Chinese power. To make these distinctions is not to discount the problems raised by Anderson, recently echoed by Jamie Merchant in the *Brooklyn Rail*.[20] The IRA is undoubtedly continuous with, and woven

---

[18] Ana Swanson, David Gelles and Jim Tankersley, 'Biden to Pause New Solar Tariffs as White House Aims to Encourage Adoption', *New York Times*, 6 June 2022; Ken Rapoza, 'China Solar Companies Qualify for Benefits Under Inflation Reduction Act', *Forbes*, 24 February 2023; Sebrina Fichtner, 'Solar Projects Using Cells from China Can Apply for IRA Subsidies', *Solarbe*, 16 May 2023.
[19] Swanson et al., 'Biden to Pause New Solar Tariffs'.
[20] Jamie Merchant, 'The Economic Consequences of Neo-Keynesianism', *Brooklyn Rail*, July–August 2023.

into, generalized hawkishness towards China, and plays on the economic nationalism that has always cohabited with and underwritten American international ambition. If Anderson overstates the climate left's silence over the domestication of the anti-China turn and broader efforts to arm for renewed American dominance, his call for the left to respond more seriously to these developments remains valid. Doing so, however, requires careful attention to the 'logics' in play—including many that have received less attention than they deserve.

Beyond the capitalist core

Tellingly, the legislation has proved most upsetting to the European Union and South Korea—'friends' whose interests the Biden Administration has decided it can afford to scant (although companies like Volkswagen, BMW and Enel are expanding their operations in the US to take advantage of the IRA's subsidies). The real global losers from the IRA are likely to be the developing countries that are already locked out of high 'value-added' sectors of industrial production and which cannot hope to compete with the major powers' capacity to self-subsidize. For much of the world, then, the 'green transition' threatens to play out like the Covid response writ large: huge spending packages in the rich world to develop cutting-edge technologies, which poor countries may eventually be permitted to buy. It is possible that US–China competition will lead both countries to court emerging markets with better terms than they might offer otherwise—but the latter will still be in the position of buyers supporting production in richer countries. That the centrality of private capital in 'green finance' globally is likely to put decarbonization projects in developing countries at the mercy of fickle investors, as Advait Arun points out, only makes matters worse.[21]

A focus on the major industrial powers should not occlude the broader shake-up of world geopolitics underway as a result of the green transition. Energy is, to put it mildly, a big deal: the input to all production in the global economy, and key to maintaining the living standards of the general population. Outside of a few exceptionally oil-rich nations, which can enjoy the benefits of high market prices while ensuring their own populations are buffered from them, most states have a strong interest in ensuring energy prices remain low. It is hardly surprising that they would take an active role in trying to ensure the reliability of

[21] Advait Arun, 'The Investment Climate', *Phenomenal World*, 26 August 2023.

energy supply and distribution, and thus in developing and protecting new energy sources. These dynamics will not disappear with fossil fuels (a development which is not, in any case, imminent), and revamping the global energy system will have significant long-run impacts for political power across the globe. Factories making EVs and batteries can, in theory, be built anywhere—but wind turbines and solar panels cannot. Similarly, the location and accelerated securitization of resources necessary for green technologies, such as lithium and rare earth minerals, is redrawing the geopolitical map.[22] Providing 'raw materials' has long been a rotten deal for countries forced to depend on the export of primary commodities—although the recent surge of global interest has given resource-rich states at least some leverage.

More generally, the shifting global order is producing a genuinely new conjuncture in climate politics, which demands rethinking in its own right. International climate agreements have long languished in the shadow of global trade, as highly publicized but largely impotent afterthoughts rather than centres of gravity in what Rosa Luxemburg called the 'world-political constellation'. Within the official institutions of global climate governance, the US has repeatedly undermined legally binding agreements even while foisting disingenuous market solutions on the rest of the planet. In response, the left has tended to simultaneously criticize both the lack of US leadership and the limits of the UN Framework Convention on Climate Change (UNFCCC) and the Conference of the Parties (COP) that gathers annually to fiddle idly with it. The political scientist Jessica Green, for example, has recently called for climate activists to pivot from climate agreements to intervening in international trade and finance.[23]

Now, however, it is the US government that is taking climate policy into the realm of trade by daring the World Trade Organization to respond to its increasingly open defiance of the same neoliberal commandments it had until recently deemed inviolable. This has glaringly exposed one of the more interesting and overlooked dynamics at the heart of the complex pairing of concerns about China and the climate: the legitimation of a mode of state capitalism that would have been unthinkable in the inner circles of American policymaking a few years ago. While this

---

[22] Thea Riofrancos, 'The Security–Sustainability Nexus: Lithium Onshoring in the Global North', *Global Environmental Politics*, vol. 23, no. 1, February 2023.
[23] Jessica Green, 'Follow the Money', *Foreign Affairs*, 12 November 2021.

development has been noted, its significance remains underexplored. For many years, the US–UK–EU drove a process of market creep outwards from the capitalist core. We are not the first to see in this change of course an increasingly powerful reciprocal influence of state capitalism on formerly dyed-in-the-wool free marketeers across the capitalist world, not only in the US, Canada and Europe, but also in Brazil, India and elsewhere. Flagship 'Bidenomics' speeches by the President and National Security Adviser Jake Sullivan have signalled what has been called the onset of 'neo-mercantilism'—the notion that China's massive subsidization programme (or Russia's state-sponsored energy industry) means they have no choice but to play the state-capitalist game.[24]

As Lola Seaton notes, the term 'political capitalism' has been used in different ways, including by the economist Branko Milanović to describe the form of capitalism on display in China and elsewhere. Milanović's definition of the term, although quite unlike Riley and Brenner's, is illuminating here. Reversing the classical Marxist view, Milanović argues that communism laid the foundations for political capitalism by building infrastructure, educating populations and creating functional states. Insofar as the capitalist 'West' is now adopting a more robust state-led approach, it suggests a striking dialectic of capitalist development: perhaps communism not only laid the foundations for the emergence of capitalism in the 'East', but now underpins efforts to revive capitalism in the 'West'?[25] If this does not necessarily augur an entirely new 'regime of accumulation', it does serve as a reminder that neoliberalism should not be conflated with capitalism: the ideological strictures of the former do not always align with the expedient pragmatism of the latter.

Missed targets?

Far less discussed is whether or not 'Bidenomics' can be meaningfully described as climate policy. The Administration claims that it is 'on track' to reduce carbon emissions 40 per cent below 2005 levels by 2030 (compared to a previous estimate of reductions coming to just under 30 per cent).[26] Many progressive organizations have endorsed

---

[24] 'Remarks by National Security Adviser Jake Sullivan on Renewing American Economic Leadership at the Brookings Institution', 27 April 2023; 'Remarks by President Biden on his Vision for the Economy', 20 April 2023.
[25] Branko Milanović, *Capitalism, Alone*, Cambridge MA 2019, pp. 67–128.
[26] 'New OMB Analysis: The Inflation Reduction Act Will Significantly Cut the Social Costs of Climate Change', Office of Management and Budget, 23 August 2022.

this optimistic claim: the Economic Policy Institute, for example, celebrated the IRA as a 'real climate change policy', one that provides 'a genuine chance at securing a liveable planet for future generations'.[27] But its shortcomings as a policy to drive down carbon emissions are well-canvassed. Manchin's decisive role in the IRA's passage means that it relies almost entirely on incentives for investments in green tech, with no direct mechanisms for reducing fossil fuel use (the bill even stipulates that in order to lease federal land for renewable energy projects, land must be offered for oil and gas development too). This theory of transition presupposes that cheaper renewables will displace fossil fuels, yet every previous energy 'transition' has actually been a process of energy addition: wood plus coal, coal plus oil, oil plus solar. There are some indications that the Administration aims to deploy the regulatory state more effectively: the Environmental Protection Agency, for example, earlier this year proposed 'the toughest-ever' standards for tailpipe emissions.[28] But absent measures to curb fossil fuel use directly, there is little to distinguish the IRA's 'carrots-only' strategy from Obama's notorious 'all of the above' energy policy. Calculations of the bill's effects also assume the widespread deployment of unproven 'negative emission' technologies such as carbon capture and storage (this is also true of some of the IPCC modelling paths, and indeed of most net-zero models). Assessing the IRA's impact on carbon emissions is made more difficult, moreover, by the fact that no one is sure quite how large it is. The most widely circulated spending number is the Congressional Budget Office's estimate of $369 billion, spread over ten years—half the *annual* budget of the US military.[29] But the lack of caps on tax credits means that spending might vastly exceed this—Tim Sahay has memorably described it as a 'bottomless mimosas' brunch for green capital and consumers.[30]

The bill's limits are not only a matter of scale. As the economist Daniela Gabor argues, the IRA's 'de-risking' approach, through which the state

---

[27] Josh Bivens, 'The Inflation Reduction Act Finally Gave the US a Real Climate Change Policy', Economic Policy Institute blog, 14 August 2023.

[28] Camila Domonoske, 'The Big Reason Why the US Is Seeking the Toughest-Ever Rules for Vehicle Emissions', NPR, 12 April 2023.

[29] 'Estimated Budgetary Effects of H.R. 5376, the Inflation Reduction Act of 2022', Congressional Budget Office, 2 August 2022.

[30] Jim Tankersley and Brad Plumer, 'Companies Flock to Biden's Climate Tax Breaks, Driving Up Cost', *New York Times*, 3 May 2023; Tim Sahay, Mark Blyth and Ted Fertik, 'What Mark Blyth Got Wrong About Bidenomics and Climate Change', talk at Brown University, 3 February 2023, available on YouTube.

entices capital to make the investments deemed necessary to prevent global catastrophe, threatens to unleash a 'disorderly' decarbonization process controlled by private interests rather than public priorities. In contrast to a just transition that would provide an offramp for people and municipalities dependent on fossil-fuel industry jobs and revenues, for example, the IRA's reliance on tax credits means that, although it contains incentives for investment in so-called 'energy communities', there is no guarantee that clean energy developments will directly benefit those most threatened by a wind-down of fossil fuels.[31] And while the IRA prioritizes commodity production—solar panels, EVs—infrastructure buildout will require massive public planning and investment, far beyond what is included in the Bipartisan Infrastructure Investment and Jobs Act. Not to mention the fact that much 'green tech' is not straightforwardly green: batteries have carbon costs of their own, and the giant ones needed for electric F-150s all the more so. The larger American vehicles are, the more lithium and other necessary resources they will use, reducing their availability for other clean energy projects and slowing the overall pace of decarbonization.[32]

At the same time, the often overlooked fact that non-profit entities, including state and municipal governments, are also eligible for tax credits (in the form of direct payments from the federal government) is significant: it represents perhaps the only opportunity for genuine public investment. The potential of this provision is illustrated by New York's recently passed Build Public Renewables Act. Championed by a coalition of socialist electoral activists and energy-sector unions, the bill requires the New York Power Authority—the largest state public utility in the country—to generate all of its electricity from clean energy by 2030, and to wind down the six natural gas plants it operates across New York City.[33]

Many have worried about the repercussions of rising US–China tension for cooperation on climate goals, and the ripple effects on the potential for

---

[31] J. Mijin Cha, 'The Future of the Labour–Climate Alliance', *Dissent*, Spring 2023; Madeleine Ngo, 'The Energy Transition Is Underway. Fossil Fuel Workers Could Be Left Behind', *NYT*, 12 July 2023.

[32] Thea Riofrancos et al., 'Achieving Zero Emissions with More Mobility and Less Mining', Climate and Community Project Report, January 2023.

[33] Aliya Uteuova, 'New York Takes Big Step Toward Renewable Energy in "Historic" Climate Win', *Guardian*, 3 May 2023.

global agreement. John Kerry's fruitless visit to Beijing in July certainly seems to bode ill. The idea animating such anxieties is that progress can happen only when major parties agree to joint reductions, because the climate crisis is ultimately a 'collective action problem' rooted in the tragedy of the commons. At least some evidence suggests, however, that countries often continue to make climate commitments in the absence of global coordination, and that climate action is more strongly driven by domestic distributive concerns than by international relations.[34] In any case, we should be able to condemn aggression towards China without needing to overstate its consequences for climate progress.

The fact remains, however, that progress on decarbonization is exceedingly hard to assess. Can the US climate movement hold the Administration to account on this front? The portrait of the American left that emerges from some of the contributions to the 'Seven Theses' debate—class-amnesiacs mired in the pernicious dynamics of secular stagnation (Riley and Brenner), or ingénues who in their ecological myopia have uncritically accepted the escalation of hostility toward China (Anderson)—might surprise the Democrats who have been haranguing climate activists for insufficient gratitude. Many of the environmental and climate-justice groups the Biden Administration initially courted with promises to devote 40 per cent of Build Back Better benefits to 'disadvantaged communities' ultimately refused to endorse the IRA, instead issuing a rebuke to the Administration. Ecosocialists have denounced the handouts to the private sector and questioned the legislation's reliability as a basis for decarbonization at speed. Youth climate activists have condemned the IRA's fossil fuel concessions and the Administration's decision to permit ConocoPhillips to drill at its 'Willow Project' in the Alaska Oil Reserve.[35]

While the left has been less quiescent than is sometimes suggested, however, the sobering reality is that such protests have had little effect.

---

[34] Michaël Aklin and Matto Mildenberger, 'Prisoners of the Wrong Dilemma: Why Distributive Conflict, Not Collective Action, Characterizes the Politics of Climate Change', *Global Environmental Politics*, vol. 20, no. 4, November 2020.
[35] Yessenia Funes, 'The Fight to Stop the Inflation Reduction Act's Fossil Fuel Giveaway', *The Frontline*, 10 August 2022; Branko Marcetic, 'The Inflation Reduction Act Should Be Cause for Relief, Not Celebration', *Jacobin*, 8 August 2022; Julia Mueller, 'Climate Activists Call on Biden to Take More Forceful Action', *the Hill*, 27 August 2023.

While the left helped to put climate change on the mainstream political agenda, its ambivalent success has taken the wind out of its own sails. White House overtures to the left wing of the Democratic Party were long ago eclipsed by efforts to bring centrists and capital in line. Yet if the ecological left has struggled to achieve its more ambitious goals, accusations of geopolitical naïveté and shoulder-shrugging about the constraints of the 'long downturn' misallocate responsibility.

A deafening silence

If Bidenomics' significance as a climate policy has been at best sub-merged in the 'Seven Theses' debate, the accelerating material impacts of global heating itself have gone almost unmentioned. The contribu-tions thus far extensively consider structural obstacles to growth of a familiar kind—overcapacity, faltering profitability, declining investment, and so on. In a follow-up article for *Sidecar* on the collapse of Silicon Valley Bank earlier this year, Riley suggested that the 're-shoring' of EV and solar panels production will eventually run up against the problems that currently plague global manufacturing as a whole:

> Imagine, for the sake of argument, that Bidenomics in its most ambitious form were successful. What exactly would this mean? Above all it would lead to the onshoring of industrial capacity in both chip manufacturing and green tech. But that process would unfold in a global context in which all the other capitalist powers were vigorously attempting to do more or less the same thing. The consequence of this simultaneous industrialization drive would be a massive exacerbation of the problems of overcapacity on a world scale.[36]

That may well be so. American car-making is emblematic of the postwar boom now uneasily shadowed by the Great Acceleration; even in the most optimistic scenario, it is hard to imagine the industry returning to its former heights or anchoring a similar round of prosperity. But this is not a convincing reason not to make these investments in the first place. It will certainly be a problem for green capital if, in another ten or twenty years, growth rates in clean-energy sectors have significantly slowed. But it's difficult to see why this should discourage us from invest-ment—even overinvestment—in low-carbon technologies. Capitalism may be 'running out of steam', as Aaron Benanav argues—though some

---

[36] Dylan Riley, 'Drowning in Deposits', NLR–*Sidecar*, 4 April 2023.

humility on this point is warranted—but it does not seem to be doing so quickly enough to prevent 'global boiling'.[37] Any future socialist project, moreover, will need batteries and solar panels, even if they are built and deployed in radically different ways.

What we want to draw attention to here, however, is a point made briefly in Thomas Meaney's analysis of the Inflation Reduction Act, but otherwise curiously missing from the discussion about the future of growth: the prospect of 'extreme events' or tipping points at various scales that could seriously disrupt or even destabilize capitalist industries and economies.[38] This silence, too, mirrors that of mainstream discourse, which still imagines a short- to medium-term in which the impacts of climate change do not yet require sustained attention—at least in the rich part of the world. But it is hardly alarmist to point out that the decline of manufacturing profitability and the dynamics of 'political capitalism'— preventing what Riley and Brenner call 'the construction of hegemonic growth coalitions'—are not the only important limits to the possibilities for future growth. A changed and increasingly volatile climate is now a guaranteed feature of any future we can imagine. The utility of economic forecasts or political diagnoses that don't factor this volatility, and its potentially cataclysmic effects, into their premises is significantly diminished. The repression of the material significance of present and future climate change is symptomatic of the refusal to recognize the climate as a political force in its own right.

A truly epochal crisis may not be on the immediate horizon—although it would only take a few consecutive firestorm summers like 2023 to have a significant impact on, say, tourism and agriculture in southern Europe. But the possibility of more contained yet severe effects is increasing, as climate change reverberates back into 'the economy' via turmoil in insurance markets, the depletion of major aquifers, urban 'natural' disasters, or any number of other shocks. Private insurers have recently stopped offering homeowner policies in California and Florida, two of the largest states in the US, both vulnerable to extreme weather.[39]

---

[37] Benanav, 'A Dissipating Glut?'; Ajit Niranjan, '"Era of Global Boiling Has Arrived", Says UN Chief as July Set to Be Hottest Month on Record', *Guardian*, 27 July 2023.
[38] Thomas Meaney, 'Fortunes of the Green New Deal', NLR 138, Nov–Dec 2022, p. 99.
[39] 'Climate Change Is Coming for America's Property Market', *Economist*, 21 September 2023. Hurricanes in Florida last year cost the state between 7.5 per cent and 10 per cent of its GDP.

Major American urban centres are at risk of running out of fresh water: in June 2023, the governor of Arizona announced a ban on real estate development in areas of Phoenix that rely on groundwater and cannot guarantee adequate supplies—a drop in the bucket in light of the fact that the Colorado River is running dry.[40] Catastrophic flooding and drought have decimated crops around the world, including rice, a staple food for much of the global population. Its paddy fields having been submerged by heavy monsoon rains, India—which exports 40 per cent of the world's rice—in July announced a ban on some exports, sparking fears of a global food crisis.[41] Agricultural total factor productivity growth has also declined significantly since mid-century as a result of climate change.[42] Actuaries are now echoing scientists' panicked warnings that low estimates of climate risk are wildly unrealistic. While extreme weather events garner the most attention, the more mundane effects of heat on labour productivity in sectors ranging from construction to meatpacking threaten to exacerbate both low productivity growth and public health emergencies worldwide.

Many economists remain remarkably sanguine about the prospects of growth amidst global warming. Nobel Prize-winner William Nordhaus infamously estimated that 3° of warming—more than double what we have experienced so far—would reduce global GDP by just 2.1 per cent, while even 6° of warming—approximately the difference between current temperatures and those of the Ice Age—would reduce GDP by only 8 per cent.[43] Gernot Wagner and Martin Weitzman's analysis of 'climate shocks', by contrast—which thus far appears more in line with observed reality—suggests that 6° of warming might reduce output by 30 per cent but very possibly a great deal more.[44] A scenario where impacts are so severe as to undercut capital accumulation altogether would constitute the kind of 'second contradiction' of capitalism long discussed

---

[40] Jeremy Childs and Ian James, 'Water Concerns Prompt New Limits on Growth in Arizona', *Los Angeles Times*, 1 June 2023.

[41] Rajendra Jadhav, Mayank Bhardwaj and Shivam Patel, 'India Imposes Major Rice Export Ban, Triggering Inflation Fears', *Reuters*, 20 July 2023.

[42] Ariel Ortiz-Bobea et al., 'Anthropogenic Climate Change Has Slowed Global Agricultural Productivity Growth', *Nature Climate Change*, no. 11, April 2021.

[43] William Nordhaus, 'Climate Change: The Ultimate Challenge for Economics', *American Economic Review*, vol. 109, no. 6, June 2019.

[44] Gernot Wagner and Martin Weitzman, *Climate Shock: The Economic Consequences of a Hotter Planet*, Princeton 2016, p. 62.

by thinkers like James O'Connor, and more recently, Nancy Fraser and Jason Moore.[45]

Politics in a warming world

What do such climate shocks portend for politics—and for 'political capitalism'? As Seaton observes, it is possible to imagine that a zero-sum economy, rather than pitching workers against each other and exacerbating intra-class antagonisms, would instead intensify class struggle; the idea that growth defers distributive conflict is one of the few things on which capitalism's advocates and critics can agree. But even stagnation—or the 'steady state' long envisioned by ecological economists—now seems a disconcertingly optimistic scenario in view of the profound instability and negative-sum dynamics likely to be set in motion by climate-related shocks. Even if extreme climate impacts do not generate major economic ripple effects in the near-term, they will be felt in daily life as people lose their homes to disasters, are forced to work outside amid life-threatening heat waves, and so on. As catastrophic and deadly as some of these events may be, many will not pose imminent threats to accumulation. It is impossible to imagine that there will be *no* eventual economic repercussions of a warming climate, even if they do not become significant for a time—but the sorry fact is that capitalism is clearly able to continue and even thrive in the face of vast human suffering.

The idea that capitalism will ultimately collapse under the weight of its ecological contradictions is too simplistic, and may be too optimistic. At present, Bidenomics is a more traditional economic programme than one might expect in response to an ostensibly existential threat: it does not anticipate and seek to address the novel problems—crop failures, severe water shortages, mass displacement—that climate change will increasingly throw at us. But states are hardly likely to stand idly by as capitalism undercuts its own future prospects. Elite concern about climate change is motivated not only by concern for the natural environment, but by

---

[45] James O'Connor, 'Capitalism, Nature, Socialism: A Theoretical Introduction', *Capitalism, Nature, Socialism*, vol. 1, no. 1, 1988; Nancy Fraser, 'Climates of Capital: For a Trans-Environmental Eco-Socialism', NLR 127, Jan–Feb 2021; Jason Moore, *Capitalism in the Web of Life: Ecology and the Accumulation of Capital*, London and New York 2015.

worry about the effects of warming on political life and on the economy. State efforts to spur green investment can be understood in part as efforts to coordinate a response to capital's self-destructive tendencies—efforts which are internally divided and contradictory, like capital itself.[46] If the effects of climate change begin to take their toll on the economy, however, efforts to nurture a successor to fossil capitalism are likely to accelerate. The 'slow violence' of climate impacts, too, will reshape the political landscape as states are increasingly called upon to respond to knock-on effects—whether by stepping in to fill the gap left by private insurers or supplying recovery funds to communities hit by disaster.[47]

The growing impact of climate shocks, in other words, will likely necessitate ever more state intervention to guarantee the conditions for accumulation on the one hand, and secure some degree of popular legitimacy amid climate chaos on the other. As dire as this prospect is, it also offers opportunities for contestation from the left. James O'Connor once suggested that ecological problems might offer a 'second path' to eco-socialism, as capitalism not only socialized the means of production but demanded increasingly socialized responses to capitalist destruction.[48] We need not accept this logic entirely to recognize the potentially productive tensions generated by scenarios in which the state's role grows as ecological crises escalate, opening up directly political battles over the nature and purpose of investment.[49]

It is of course impossible to anticipate precisely what the political repercussions of a changing climate will be. For all the immediacy of a heatwave or flood, climate change remains a heavily mediated phenomenon. Although some discern opportunities for progressive forces in a post-carbon economy, there is no reason to assume that the social

---

[46] Alyssa Battistoni, 'State, Capital, Nature: State Theory for the Capitalocene', in Rob Hunter, Rafael Khachaturian and Eva Nanopoulos, eds, *Marxism and the Capitalist State: Towards a New Debate*, London 2023.

[47] Rob Nixon, *Slow Violence and the Environmentalism of the Poor*, Cambridge MA and London 2011.

[48] O'Connor, '*Capitalism, Nature, Socialism*: A Theoretical Introduction'.

[49] Popular control of investment is a key theme of Aaron Benanav's contribution to the debate. He argues that a low-carbon society oriented towards meeting human needs implies 'a thoroughgoing democratization of the investment process and its function, not only for legitimacy, but for ensuring the right outcomes': Benanav, 'A Dissipating Glut', p. 80.

and political consequences of a hotter planet will benefit the left.[50] A zero-sum world might intensify class conflict, but it might just as easily inflame other social divisions. As Mike Davis foresaw over a decade ago—'selective adaptation for Earth's first-class passengers' and 'the creation of green and gated oases of permanent affluence on an otherwise stricken planet'—the urban rich are presently protecting themselves from water scarcity by depriving the poor, while climate migration threatens to aggravate already-heightened xenophobia.[51]

As essential as it is to remain vigilant about these possibilities, however, it is equally vital to question their inevitability. One of capitalism's most profound ideological effects has been to naturalize the expectation that a zero-sum state is necessarily a Hobbesian one; projecting present arrangements into the future without qualification or criticism naturally produces dystopian, even apocalyptic expectations. Certainly it is crucial to consider, as many contributions to the 'Seven Theses' debate have done, the long-term, structural constraints on capitalism's dynamism. But resigned warnings about the grim prospects of a low-growth future risk hastening, rather than refusing, the fate that awaits us in a zero-sum world. Challenging this common sense and highlighting points of potential solidarity instead seems to us to be one of the fundamental premises of left politics. Glimpses of promising political developments are beginning to appear. During this year's 'hot labour summer', climate-related issues began to shape labour politics beyond the familiar fields of energy: UPS workers demanded and won air conditioning in trucks, and Amazon warehouse workers walked out when forced to work in excessive heat. Whether these demands for the kinds of adaptation measures necessary for survival in a warmer world can successfully be translated into demands for more aggressive mitigation remains to be seen. But they represent, at the very least, a step towards integrating ecological issues into political projects of all kinds—and doing so not only through technocratic initiatives or even efforts to assemble coalitions around 'interests', but through demands from below.

---

[50] Pierre Charbonnier has argued that decarbonization may transform politics in ways that favour the left, allowing it to 'repoliticize needs': 'Ouvrir la brèche: politique du monde post-carbone', *Le Grand Continent*, 14 June 2021.
[51] Mike Davis, 'Who Will Build the Ark?', NLR 61, Jan–Feb 2010, p. 38; Elisa Savelli et al., 'Urban Water Crises Driven by Elites' Unsustainable Consumption', *Nature Sustainability*, no. 6, April 2023.

We agree with Riley and Brenner that 'time-worn shibboleths and old patterns of thought' are inadequate—but this is just as true of left analyses that neglect the climate. There is no future in which climate change will not impinge on all political questions. Climate is reshaping the terrain on which we will be fighting in the years to come, and we have only begun to consider what this will mean. Perhaps the most hopeful thing one might say about Bidenomics at this moment is that it is a mumbled, reluctant recognition of this fact, and we should be grateful for those who have fought so hard to force the matter, even if we are still so very, very far from where we need to go.

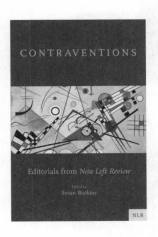

Matters II

by Max Winter
New edition, translations
and transposition.

Matters II tells the brutal, fragmented tale of two people trapped in the modern service proletariat. Greta and Gregor Matters endure an everyday reality that routinely ravages their fragile hopes and desperate efforts to create an illusion in which they can survive. The topic of the „Working Poor" is highlighted by the translations in the appropriate supra-national, location-independent, and multilingual dimension.

The American translation has also been further developed into a de-localized adaptation, with one version taking place in Vienna, as in the original text, and another transferred to New York. However, in the Hungarian translation relocating the story to Budapest, although only 250 km away from Vienna, was not as straightforward. Therefore, the Hungarian translation is only available as a traditional translation.

Matters II
2. Auflage 2023 – E◇1
ISBN 978-3-903401-01-3
101 nummerierte
Exemplare.
€15,00

Matters II
Translated and transposed
by Paul David Young
1. Edition 2023 – E◇3
ISBN 978-3-903401-03-7
Edition of 101 numbered copies.
$16,50, £13,00

Mattersék
Fordította Péter Mesés
1. Kiadás 2023 – E◇2
ISBN 978-3-903401-02-0
101 számozott példány.
HUF 3900,00

www.raute.cc

VIENNA

JOHANNES HOERNING

THINKING THE UNTHINKABLE

The Political Philosophy of Ci Jiwei

I N HIS 1989–92 lecture series *On the State* Pierre Bourdieu, following Durkheim, proposed a provisional definition of the state as the basis for 'both the logical and the moral conformity of the social world'. By 'logical conformity', Bourdieu meant that the agents of the social world would share the same categories of perception, the same construction of reality; by 'moral conformity', their agreement on certain core values. Taking his distance from classical state theory, such as that of Hobbes or Locke—in which the state, occupying a quasi-godlike viewpoint, oversees all and serves the common good—as also from Marxian traditions, from Gramsci to Althusser and beyond, which focus on the function of the state as an apparatus for maintaining public order in the interests of the ruling bloc, Bourdieu emphasized instead the need to grasp the 'organizational magic' of the state as a principle of consciousness—its monopoly of legitimate *symbolic* as well as physical violence. The social theorist therefore needed to be particularly on guard against Durkheimian 'pre-notions' or received ideas, against 'thinking the state with state thinking'. A first step was to conceive the state as what Bourdieu called 'an almost unthinkable object'.[1]

If there is one thinker who has met Bourdieu's challenge to 'think the state' without succumbing to 'state thinking', it is the Chinese political philosopher Ci Jiwei. Recently retired from the philosophy department of the University of Hong Kong, Ci has devoted most of the past three decades to analysing the nature and evolution of China's state and society since the founding of the People's Republic in 1949. Three of his four books—*Dialectic of the Chinese Revolution* (1994), *Moral China in the Age of Reform* (2014) and *Democracy in China* (2019)—amount to a loose trilogy aiming to clarify the 'logic' of the Chinese experience and to track the evolution of the CCP regime since Mao. The collapse of Maoist utopianism and the liberalization of the economy after 1978 have left Chinese society in a 'fundamentally unsettled' condition, Ci argues.[2] Each book in the trilogy addresses a different symptom of this situation: existential or social-psychological malaise in *Dialectic of the Chinese Revolution*, the undermining of moral subjectivity in *Moral China* and the looming crisis of political legitimacy in *Democracy in China*. In different ways, they are all concerned with how the Chinese party-state might accommodate itself, for its own and the nation's good, to citizens' need to act freely and to understand themselves as free, while at the same time preserving its own stability and that of the country at large.[3]

On a superficial reading, Ci's concern with democracy and the state might seem to situate him in the company of conventional liberals, while his emphasis on the Party's role might appear to class him with loyal defenders of the CCP. Such interpretations would miss both the originality of his political philosophy and the radical-popular character of his proposals, which in his most recent book are frankly democratic socialist. Ci occupies an unusual insider-outsider position, in both East and West: professionally established in the PRC, yet situated on its rimland, with only a small section of his *oeuvre* published in Chinese; deeply informed by Western traditions of critical political philosophy, including Marxist ones, as well as Chinese approaches, yet not in or of the West. What follows will trace the development of Ci's thought against the backdrop of the PRC's evolution, drawing out some of its key political-philosophical themes and considering some of the objections raised

---

[1] Pierre Bourdieu, *On the State: Lectures at the Collège de France, 1989–1992*, Patrick Champagne et al., eds, tr. David Fernbach, Cambridge 2014, pp. 3–4, 106–7. While these lecture notes were edited and published a decade after his death, Bourdieu's 1993 'Esprits d'État: genèse et structure du champ bureaucratique' remains his major study of the state. It should be added that Ci himself nowhere systematically links his own reflections on the state to Bourdieu's, though he has made mention of Bourdieu's work: he refers to *The Logic of Practice* in *The Two Faces of Justice*, Cambridge MA 2006, p. 145, and to Bourdieu's notion of 'symbolic capital' in the essay 'A Gloss on *Chongjian*', published in the catalogue of the group show *Reconstruction* at Karma International Zurich, 2021, curated by Aita Sulser and Johannes Hoerning.
[2] Ci Jiwei, *Democracy in China: The Coming Crisis*, Cambridge MA 2019, p. 195.
[3] Ci, *Democracy in China*, p. 227.

by his critics, with the aim of contributing to an overall evaluation of a strikingly original body of work.

I. DIAGNOSIS

Ci was born in 1955 in Beijing, where his parents were scientists at Peking University. Two years old at the onset of the anti-rightist campaign, eleven at the start of the Cultural Revolution and twenty-three when Deng Xiaoping initiated the Reform Era, he had his fair share of personal experiences, good and bad, of China's turbulent twentieth century. Living on campus exposed Ci to the turmoil of the Cultural Revolution, and he has written memorably, in general terms, of the experience of that epoch.[4] His education was disrupted by extended periods of physical labour in the countryside and immersion in peasant life; once it resumed, it was at first scarcely indicative of his personal choices, since training was still subject to a high degree of political administration. This was partly true even when Ci spent time in London (1978–9) and Edinburgh (1979–83) as a state-sponsored, indeed state-managed, student. In London, Ci studied English intensively and experienced daily life, culture and politics in a foreign country for the first time. In Edinburgh, his landlord was a primary-school teacher who happened to be a Marxist; on his shelves, Ci encountered Sartre's *Critique of Dialectical Reason*, Thompson's *The Making of the English Working Class* and Marcuse's *One-Dimensional Man*. He also came to know the writings of Russell, Freud and Weber, the philosophy of Hume, Wittgenstein and Popper, the moral philosophy of Adam Smith and R. M. Hare, the linguistics of Chomsky and M. A. K. Halliday, the fiction of George Eliot, Henry James and Iris Murdoch, and the literary criticism of Auerbach and Leavis. This wide reading would leave its mark on his reflections on Chinese society and politics.

Ci left China on a visit to the US in April 1989—he would spend 1990–91 as a fellow at the Stanford Humanities Center—and thus by coincidence,

---

[4] As Ci would recall of the GPCR: 'Fear of being wrong is equivalent to fear of punishment, for every political wrong brings punishment in the form of persecution. And by the same token the urge to be right derives from the same motive, as the urge to mete out rather than to receive punishment. To be right is to have the right to persecute. Small wonder that one remembers certain political dogmas as one remembers laws prohibiting theft and murder': *Dialectic of the Chinese Revolution: From Utopianism to Hedonism*, Stanford 1994, p. 89.

like many Chinese scholars and students abroad, he found himself in the vast shadow cast by the events of 4 June, watching from afar. *Dialectic of the Chinese Revolution* was conceived, as Ci recalls in the book's introduction, 'amid the sadness, anger and sense of futility in the wake of the suppression of the democracy movement'. Drafted at Stanford and then at the National Humanities Center in North Carolina (1991–92), it was a way to come to terms with the events, and in particular with what had happened (or failed to happen) in their aftermath. Ci explains, in a rather personal tone that is rare in his work, 'As the nation's mood went from shock to despair and then, remarkably soon, from despair to business as usual, I sensed, in a way I had never quite done before, something profoundly wrong with the Chinese spirit, something whose nature and cause had to be sought at the deepest level of the Chinese experience.' His objective was at once one 'of understanding myself and of illuminating, with my very limited powers, an entire epoch'.[5]

Dialectic of the Chinese Revolution can be read as a kind of genealogy of this spiritual malaise, set in a deeper comparative and historical framework which allows contrasts between the abandonment of Maoist ideology and the earlier discarding of Confucianism. It is also an attempt, as Ci puts it, to chart 'the path traversed by Chinese consciousness' from the optimistic founding of the PRC in 1949 and the exalted asceticism under Mao to the still-reverberating consequences of the demise of that 'utopian experiment'. As Ci writes: 'Utopian consciousness, once aroused, had a momentum that would not rest content until its original basis, the crisis of the body, was overcome, until its hopes were either fulfilled or dashed.' The dashing of those hopes resulted in a devastating loss of meaning and of belief in the future—that 'most precious mental possession'—and ushered in a pervasive spirit of nihilism. The acquisitive individualism encouraged by China's spectacular rise was a way of numbing or burying this experience of meaninglessness—not merely meaning's absence, but the anguish of its disappearance. Ci reads the psychological crisis of the Reform Era—the demise of communist utopianism as mass psychological reality—in terms of a crisis of spirit (*jingshen weiji*) or of belief (*xinyang weiji*). Consumerist pleasure-seeking was a technique of oblivion: a way for a 'spiritually exhausted people' to endure nihilism, 'without raising it to the level of conscious reflection'.[6]

---

[5] Ci, *Dialectic of the Chinese Revolution*, pp. 2, 20–23.
[6] Ci, *Dialectic of the Chinese Revolution*, pp. 2, 207, 169, 226, 11, 6. Bafflingly, as Ci puts it, the upshot of domestic tyranny after June 4 was 'mental colonization by a foreign ideology [consumerism]': p. 89.

Ci is concerned here with Chinese culture in the broadest sense: struc-tures of experience and meaning; moral systems; the changing common sense of what China is, in itself and relative to the rest of the world. With the shock of the 1839–42 Opium War, he notes, a culture that had, for 2,000 years, been entirely sure of itself—its impregnable sovereignty, acknowledged superiority to neighbouring states and relative isolation from the rest of the world underpinning its 'centre mentality'—was obliged to come to terms with the military and technological para-mountcy of an industrial Western power. China's response to this profound cultural crisis was to repurpose an ancient metaphysical dis-tinction between being and doing as a national strategy: *zhongxue weiti, xixue weiyong*—'Chinese learning as essence (*ti*), Western learning as technique (*yong*)'. The *ti-yong* formula relegated the humiliating need to adopt foreign technologies to the realm of cultural insignificance. Yet the need for such distinctions signalled that the integrity of Chinese culture had already been undermined, Ci argues; it could no longer evolve on its own terms, at its own pace, and so could no longer be the China it had always been; but nor could it be quite like the West. Maoism resolved the disjunction: after 1949, Beijing regained complete sovereignty over the mainland for the first time since the 1840s; the PRC acquired a new cos-mopolitan identity at the forefront of history, continuous with what Mao described as the 'good part' of Chinese tradition and as culturally distinc-tive as it had ever been. The exhaustion of Maoist utopianism brought new uncertainty about the relation of *ti* and *yong*, however; the only faith capable of replacing it would be patriotism, Ci suggested, though that would be a poor substitute except under conditions of war.

Following a structure at once loose and intricate—a hallmark of Ci's works—the book's six chapters do not comprise a continuous account, though they are approximately chronological. Instead, each tracks the evolving relations and logical connections among Ci's key terms—utopianism, hedonism, nihilism—along with several other subsidiary concepts, including asceticism, collectivism, altruism and liberalism, which serve to nuance and embroider the general historical move-ment he traces from utopianism to hedonism via nihilism. Despite its ascetic aspect, Maoist utopianism contained a 'sublimated' hedonism—its promise of well-being for all in a communist future was hedonism postponed. Once that future failed to materialize, the utopian energies that had been stoked by it were instead channelled into market hedon-ism. Yet an element of utopianism was 'preserved in nihilism', which bears the marks of utopianism's 'exacting standards'—its heightened consciousness and accentuated future—precisely in the depths of its disappointment and despair.[7]

Reciprocal corruptions

As he was formulating the ideas that made up *Dialectic of the Chinese Revolution*, it became clear to Ci that he would not be able to publish them in China. Instead of seeking an alternative publisher in Taiwan, however, he decided to wait until things changed on the mainland. That day has yet to arrive, and it may be that it has receded further than ever. At no point, however, has Ci been moved to exchange his perspective on the present for what Walter Benjamin called the 'comfortable view of the past'. In 1997 he took up a position teaching political philosophy at the University of Hong Kong. His second book, *The Two Faces of Justice*, was published in China in 2001 and appeared in English in 2006. Unlike his other works, in which theoretical reflections are explicitly situated in an analysis of Chinese society and politics, *The Two Faces of Justice* is a more abstract inquiry into what Ci terms 'the logic of the sociali- zation of justice', and its contemporary applications are more implicit. Nonetheless, by clarifying the social conditions under which people are willing to behave justly—the state-mediated, psychological mecha- nisms through which justice is 'socialized'—the book touches on many of the core concerns of the China trilogy, including the human need for a sense of agency and autonomy, the state's role in enforcing conform- ity and maintaining social stability, and the circumstances under which these break down.[8]

When justice is successfully socialized, people come to think of their disposition to follow moral norms as unconditional. For Ci, this self- understanding is a form of misrecognition, since the willingness to behave justly is in fact intrinsically conditional, because it is a 'socially

---

[7] Arif Dirlik's short review of *Dialectic of the Chinese Revolution* for the *American Historical Review*, while sympathetic to the work's 'controlled anger', signally mis- construed Ci's trenchant psychological diagnosis as 'blaming the victims'. He would surely have revised this judgement had he been able to see the future course of Ci's work. Arif Dirlik, 'Jiwei Ci, *Dialectic of the Chinese Revolution: From Utopianism to Hedonism*', *American Historical Review*, April 1996, pp. 540–41.

[8] As an early footnote reveals, Ci's interest in the 'contagious nature of injustice' had its roots in his observations of the breakdown of social obligation and reciprocity in post-Mao China, where 'the phenomenon is sometimes quite striking': Jiwei Ci, *The Two Faces of Justice*, Cambridge MA and London 2006, p. 1.

achieved virtue'. Rather than arising from independently grounded principles or natural instinct, as philosophers from Hume to MacIntyre have argued, the individual readiness to comply with moral norms is dependent on other members of the relevant group behaving likewise—in Ci's terms, 'the *reciprocal* satisfaction of interests'.[9] This is the sense in which justice is two-faced. The state is the only agent capable of enforcing the 'reciprocity condition'; its institutions of punishment (and forgiveness) are means by which it both maintains its status as the sovereign guardian of justice and ameliorates its own failure whenever people violate moral norms—whenever those norms lose their unconditional appearance, leading people to become disinclined to follow them. Lawbreaking or corruption is thus a sign that the condition of reciprocity has broken down, which in turn is an indication of the weakening authority of the state.[10]

Ci's next book, written in the early 2010s, examined the moral wasteland produced by twenty years of breakneck economic growth. *Moral China in the Age of Reform* does not focus simply on official corruption but on a more far-reaching dissolution of the ties of social reciprocity, under which 'everyday norms of coexistence and cooperation' are breached on a massive scale, such that 'it is no longer remotely alarmist to speak of the corruption of an entire people'. Ci is typically sparing with empirical detail, but he offers such concrete examples as 'unsafe food (infant formula and so-called gutter oil among the most prominent examples), medicine, water and traffic, not to mention coal mines.'[11] This generalized corruption, even if it is a common condition throughout the industrial-capitalist world, can be understood in part as an outcome of disillusion with utopian promises that demanded too much and delivered too little. But Ci also sees the stunted development of moral subjectivity as the result of a mismatch between the official 'value-infrastructure' of Chinese life and the changed socioeconomic reality on the ground. The consumer freedoms that China's proto-bourgeois subjects have enjoyed since the 1990s have not been consecrated at the level of moral culture,

---

[9] Ci, *The Two Faces of Justice*, pp. 7, 6, 232, 5.
[10] Ci, *The Two Faces of Justice*, pp. 5–6, 36.
[11] Jiwei Ci, *Moral China in the Age of Reform*, Cambridge 2014, pp. 21, 168, 15. *Moral China* combines and revises early publications by Ci in various journals. The assessment of China as undergoing a moral crisis, a foreseeable development of what he called a 'psychological crisis' in *Dialectic* (p. 100), dates back to 2008: 'The Moral Crisis in Post-Mao China: Prolegomenon to a Philosophical Analysis', *Diogenes*, vol. 56, no. 1, 2009.

where *de facto* economic and other freedoms are not 'raised to the level of a society-defining value'.[12]

Ci understands freedom not as an individual right but as a paradigm providing for the human need for agency, while also securing social order. Prior to the Reform Era, moral conformity in China—the social production of 'moral willingness'—depended not on freedom but on an alternative paradigm: identification with moral exemplars and loyalty to the leader. This loyalty was absolute, encompassing and conflating politics and morality in such a way that freedom was not a felt necessity. 'The old belief in communism', Ci writes, 'was able to reduce morality to political loyalty and happily dispense with any independently based moral agency.' Collective, future-oriented communist values 'left no place (and arguably little need) for individual liberties'.[13] Yet this conflation of morality and politics under the Maoist state was intrinsically precarious: moral authority was liable to be undermined once the political project that had legitimized it gave way. As Ci had observed in *Dialectic of the Chinese Revolution*, while Marxism had served the needs of ameliorating the country's backwardness, it did not provide a new system of moral rules or statecraft. By subsuming morality into politics, the Maoist state was instead continuing the old logic of the Confucian tradition, under which political and intellectual legitimacy were made to go 'hand in hand'.[14] The post-Mao CCP, by contrast, ever surer of its globally measurable success rate, ceased to rely on overburdening moral demands—demands, moreover, which it knew often stood in the way of market expansion. In a rapidly rising China, the political riddle at Zhongnanhai was no longer how to use one's power to serve a higher morality, but how to make morality work for one's power.

Following Deng's reforms, Ci writes, the logic of the 'individualization of everyday life' demanded the formation of an alternative, Western-style 'superego-centred morality'. But the perdurance of the PRC's undemocratic political structures kept the individual superego weak, 'denied the room to become a robust moral force'—and Ci adds: 'That room is freedom'.[15] China's incomplete

---

[12] Ci, *Moral China*, pp. 159, 210, 175, 45. The book's initial working title was *China's Lurch to Freedom*.
[13] Ci, *Moral China*, pp. 48–49, 23, 55, 207.
[14] Ci, *Dialectic*, pp. 132, 93.
[15] Ci, *Moral China*, pp. 55, 3, 121.

transition between moral paradigms—from agency-through-identifi-cation to agency-through-freedom—accompanied its as-yet-incomplete transition from a dynastic state (Legalist-Confucian, then Maoist) to a juridical one. The absence of a successor moral paradigm results not only in corruption but in a kind of intellectual incoherence. Ci discusses the Party's efforts to navigate this situation through the conceptual appa-ratus of sublimation, desublimation and resublimation, concepts trialled in *Dialectic of the Chinese Revolution*. 'Partial resublimation' is his term for the stopgap manoeuvres that aim to avert or disguise the contradic-tions of the communist twilight: the attempt to revive discourses which 'bear little relation to a *habitus,* a concrete way of life'; moral-political imperatives like 'serve the people', which were only meaningful when embedded 'in an ascetic, anti-consumerist form of life'. Invoking them in its absence produced not conformity but cynicism among Chinese citizens, who were liable to see the empty manoeuvring of official lan-guage as merely 'going through certain linguistic motions'.[16]

Completing the transition to a new paradigm of moral agency requires not a revival of moribund discourse but a real 'revolution in values'. *Moral China* is an exercise in imagining the substance of this revolu-tion. The 21st-century state has ceded responsibility for the livelihood of its citizens, meaning that Chinese people today have to fend for them-selves as individuals and are 'left to their own devices'. This has been accompanied by a levelling of values, now almost solely centred on the mundane concerns of prosperity, enjoyment and security. Ci describes this as 'populism with respect to values'—a populism that is 'substan-tive', because 'thoroughgoing', but lacking any credible procedures for registering and affirming popular preferences. This 'desublima-tion' of values—from collective future to individual prosperity—has in turn given rise to a novel idea of 'equality of agency' (quite compatible with wide quantitative inequalities in income), of a partially negative kind: equality among 'atomistic individuals who are at once (potential) bourgeois subjects and subject to the alienating, competitive capitalist order'. Indeed, the widespread resentment at corruption is itself evi-dence of the hold of 'qualitative equality, of people as equal agents and choosers' in the Chinese social imaginary. Mass resentment represents a transformation of subjectivity: people take themselves to be entitled to a certain respect.[17]

---

[16] Ci, *Moral China*, pp. 30, 77.
[17] Ci, *Moral China*, pp. 205, 161, 206–7, 112, 162–3.

The official refusal to 'valorize' the new system of values prevents the emergent bourgeoisified subject from becoming itself. Yet for Ci, the route out of this unsatisfactory limbo does not run through unqualified emulation of the Western model. Both freedom and democracy are, in Ci's thought, 'contested concepts'—spaces of experiment rather than finished artefacts to be imported wholesale from the West. Indeed Western iterations of freedom can be a species of false consciousness: an official value which helps to enforce conformity by enabling people to overrate the extent of their own autonomy—'concealing relations of domination' and the degree to which peoples' lives are in fact externally determined. Liberal political regimes are good at creating the (real) conditions under which freedom and agency are plausible illusions. The hallmark of a liberal society, Ci writes, is the 'seamless conjunction' of 'the experience of freedom' and the 'practice of conformity'.[18]

In *Moral China*'s sweeping philosophical coda—speculative reflections on human nature and modernity—Ci identifies nihilism as the key to grasping 'the spirit and dynamic of the modern world as a whole', arguing that what nihilism means above all is the demise of 'the good', as 'fit to guide and limit human conduct'. If freedom has eclipsed 'the good' in many Western democracies, the challenge and opportunity for China, where Ci argues 'the good' has historically enjoyed particular primacy, is to develop 'a bracing dialectic between liberty and the good': to affirm freedom but also to shape it, 'bringing it into positive alignment with some shared and unifying conception of the good'. China in his view has a unique chance to pioneer practices of freedom and democracy that improve upon the flawed ones available in the West, especially in protecting citizens against the injustices wrought by the unfettered market. For better or worse, the individualistic manner in which Chinese citizens now live their lives must be institutionalized: for better, if interpreted as

---

[18] Ci, *Moral China*, p. 49. In Ci's thought, the ambiguity of freedom in some ways recalls the Janus-face of justice: just as the state, through the social institution of justice, allows people to misrecognize their conditional motivations as unconditional imperatives, so the public notion of freedom is an interpretation of behaviour that allows people to think of themselves as free agents when in fact they are dominated and determined. There is thus the paradox that the full-throated espousal of freedom is often accompanied by widespread ideological conformity; 'freedom' becomes an effective means, in modern conditions, of reconciling the individual need for agency with the need for social order.

a first, necessary step toward democratic politics; for worse, if used as justification for market despotism without social protections.[19]

Programme for the Party?

If *The Two Faces of Justice* was a 'philosophical intervention' and *Moral China* 'an act of intellectual and civic intervention', Ci's most recent work, *Democracy in China*, is a pointedly political one. 'An exercise in democratic theory embedded in a discussion of China', the book's core arguments were conceived in the aftermath of Hong Kong's 2014 Umbrella protests and developed in a series of lectures Ci delivered at Harvard in late 2015. By the time it was published, the 2019 Hong Kong protests against Beijing's Extradition Bill were underway and tensions between Beijing and Washington were mounting under Trump's trade tariffs. As Ci's most concretely political book, *Democracy in China* caps a trend one can discern across the trilogy: the books have become world-lier in theme and more interventionist in orientation; in addition to Marx and Nietzsche, thinkers like Tocqueville, Polanyi, Habermas and Althusser have come to the fore.[20]

Ci furnishes a punctilious demolition of the notion that Chinese citizens neither need nor desire democracy—an illusion reinforced by the 'officially imposed moratorium' on the topic, but also bolstered by Western commentators, in what Ci characterizes as a species of 'new (political) orientalism'. He takes aim at Daniel Bell's argument that the CCP can draw its legitimacy from its impressive economic performance alone. Ci distinguishes between such 'performance legitimacy' and the 'right to rule' itself—the mandate to perform in the first place. In his theoretical schema, performance can only enhance legitimacy if there is some prior legitimacy to enhance. During the Confucian period, the mandate to rule was said to derive from heaven. Under communism, that cosmology was replaced by a 'teleological' legitimacy. This kind of legitimacy was prefigured in the CCP's founding in 1921 and the defeat of the Japanese invasion, lasting from the communist revolution of 1949

---

[19] Ci, *Moral China*, pp. 222, 219. It should be noted that giving priority to 'the good' does not entail endorsing any particular good, whether Confucian, communist or liberal capitalist.

[20] Ci, *Democracy in China*, pp. 31, 1; henceforward, DC.

through the Mao era and beyond. Bell's apolitical account fails to register that the CCP's right to rule remains inextricably tied to its revolutionary past, Ci argues. Yet this residual legitimacy is close to exhaustion: Xi Jinping represents the last credible link to the communist story and its glorious beginnings; with his eventual passing, the Party will need to find a new ideological principle, fit for the wealthier, more individualistic society over which it now rules.[21]

Ci thus urges the CCP leadership to consider the prudential case for democracy, *à la* Tocqueville, as the best way to ensure the resilience and durability of its rule. Marx himself, he notes, was 'unquestionably a democratic thinker, seeking to move beyond the bourgeois democratic revolution rather than merely opposing it.' The prudential case does not depend on normative appeals nor on Aristotelian definitions of the 'best' regime. The only goods at stake in the prudential case are regime legitimacy (Weber) or hegemony (Gramsci), and the resultant stability they ensure. It does not need to provide 'genuine democracy, whatever that may mean' but only a 'plausible and sustainable semblance' of it, defined as what is 'more or less consonant with China's present social conditions.' Though Ci is no Habermasian, there is a notable overlap here with Habermas's propositions about democracy as a form of legiti-mation rather than an *a priori* set of institutions. In *Democracy in China*, any system that has an accepted mechanism for registering popular consent—and thus bestowing general moral approval on a regime—may be considered democratic.[22]

---

[21] DC, pp. 4, 6, 7–8, 55–58, 18–19. See also Daniel Bell, *The China Model: Political Meritocracy and the Limits of Democracy*, Princeton 2015. Branko Milanović also argues that the CCP's claim to rule is legitimated only by performance—or rather, by the state's out-performing its rivals across the Pacific: 'delivering, year in year out, more goods and services than its liberal counterpart': *Capitalism, Alone: The Future of the System that Rules the World*, Cambridge MA 2019, pp. 91–96, 209.
[22] DC, pp. 8, 13, 145, 134. Habermas has described democracy as a question of 'find-ing arrangements which can ground the presumption that the basic institutions of the society and the basic political decisions would meet with the unforced agree-ment of all those involved, if they could participate, as free and equal, in discursive will-formation. Democratization cannot mean an *a priori* preference for a specific type of organization, for example, for so-called direct democracy . . . Democracies are distinguished from other systems of domination by a rational principle of legitimation and not by types of organization marked out *a priori*.' See Jürgen Habermas, *Communication and the Evolution of Society*, tr. Thomas McCarthy, Boston 1976, p. 186.

Ci's appeal to the CCP leadership's rational self-interest rests on the perceived resilience of mature democratic regimes—the best solution to the Party's dilemma of self-perpetuation. Borrowing his terms from the political philosopher Jean Hampton, he argues that these regimes' stability resides in their multiple, progressively deeper levels of consent. Citizens may be disgruntled with a government's legislative performance—the primary level—yet still affirm the legitimacy of the electoral party system, the secondary level; even if they are dissatisfied with the existing parties, they may still have faith in the system at its tertiary level, that of the overall constitution or basic law. And below this again, democracies are sustained at the deepest level by a 'politico-cultural faith in democratic rule of law as an alternative to violent conflict'. This is what gives these regimes their durability—however unpopular their rulers or flawed their electoral systems. As Ci writes,

> The advantage afforded by such *depth of structure* becomes very striking indeed if we compare this model with its Chinese counterpart . . . in the Chinese case the main and, given the fast-disappearing revolutionary legitimacy, potentially sole locus for endorsement consent (or lack thereof) is available at the primary level, that of the making of laws and policies and their implementation. That is why performance legitimacy is such a life-and-death matter.[23]

The real risk to the regime, *Democracy in China* argues, comes not from organized opposition forces, which are not allowed to exist, nor from powerful interest groups, most of whom are beneficiaries of the existing system and would 'face an uncertain future if things were to change'. The threat comes instead from the unstoppable tendencies within Chinese society towards what Ci describes, borrowing from Tocqueville's *Democracy in America*, as 'equality of conditions'. This refers not to 'quantitative' equality but to the dissolution of traditional authority relations. The patriarchal family system, with its deeply engrained Confucian principles of filial piety and subordination of the mother and children to the authority of the father, began to crumble under the egalitarianism of the Mao era and eroded further with the pragmatism and small-family policies of Deng. Today, Ci argues, the family is no longer a training ground for obedience to authority, as the striking contrast in filial disposition between the 1950s and 1990s cohorts shows. And although the hierarchy of the urban-rural divide has persisted into the Reform Era,

---

[23] DC, pp. 139–141.

it has lost all moral legitimacy. A similar dissolution of authority has taken place in the public sphere of everyday life. With the privatization of much of the economy, Chinese society has undergone a 'levelling' to the lowest common denominator of middle-class happiness—the 'populism with respect to values' discussed in *Moral China*. People pursue 'apolitical' goals of prosperity and security, in 'a spirit of personal independence', taking their own counsel instead of deferring to those above. But while the CCP has provided a high degree of 'material satisfaction'—rapid growth, rising living standards, geopolitical clout—it has failed to offer a forum for agency, 'the sense of being citizens with a credible role in shaping the life and destiny of the political community.' This is the glaring exception to the levelling of 'fixed hierarchies'.[24]

Ci recognizes that the 'equality of conditions' which Tocqueville detected in 1830s America is today defined by powerful capitalist inequalities. While China's 'so-called socialist market economy' is not purely capitalist, it has been characterized throughout the Reform Era by 'high tolerance for inequality and environmental degradation'.[25] *Democracy in China* therefore supplements Tocqueville's diagnosis with Polanyi's insight—that mass (social) democracy has historically served to provide some protection against the ravages of capitalism's 'satanic mills', albeit (to take the English case) only after the proletariat had been tamed by the Hungry Forties and triaged to produce a stratum of 'respectable' skilled workers who could lead the rest. Even if—Ci here follows Wolfgang Streeck's analysis in *Buying Time* (2014)—the West has seen a shift to less democratic, more oligarchic forms of policy-making in the neoliberal era (the rise of non-accountable central banks, the IMF, the European Commission), residual protections persist.[26] With the Reform Era, the CCP leadership has had the task of protecting Chinese society thrust upon it; yet its economic agenda makes it both less able and less motivated to carry this out. While the Party is in a more

---

[24] DC, pp. 127–8, 161, 110, 8. See also Ci Jiwei, '*Democracy in China*: Reply to My Critics', *Dao*, 2022, p. 473.

[25] Ci describes China as 'having become as capitalist as it can be, short of relinquishing its self-understanding as a socialist market economy': DC, p. 181.

[26] DC, pp. 175, 162. Ci notes that the Polanyian idea of (social) democracy as a countervailing protection against capitalism is, unfortunately, almost completely absent in China, where 'a one-sided understanding of democracy' as granting autonomy to the market and limiting the power of the state prevails. If it were cast in Polanyian terms, building on the constant calls in China for better and more equitable healthcare, education and so forth, democracy might have greater purchase: DC, p. 185.

advantageous position vis-à-vis the forces of big capital than its Western counterparts—no 'Wall Street, Silicon Valley and military-industrial complex to contend with', as yet—it faces the more insidious risk of corrupt official- and crony-capitalism growing within its own ranks, as Xi's anti-corruption campaign acknowledged.[27]

This combination—a levelled social landscape, topped by a recalcitrant political structure, with little protection against capitalism's ills and no formal outlet for the sense of agency that accrues in everyday life— makes for systemic instability that risks becoming 'ungovernable'. In this perspective, the only option for the CCP, short of maintaining an unsustainably high performance or resorting to the dead-end of intensifying repression, will be to widen and enshrine legal and intellectual freedoms, extending eventually to political ones. As a principled realist, Ci maintains that sweeping the Party aside is not an option: the CCP remains the only 'mature' political force in China and it clearly retains sufficient unity and cohesion to 'keep potentially fatal factionalism at bay and to maintain the deterrence effect of June 4 against any similar uprising.'[28] Given the balance of forces, any direct confrontation would be doomed to defeat. Democratization, in Ci's 'realistic utopia', would be spearheaded by a judicious CCP. The ground would first need to be prepared by social-justice reforms to alleviate economic inequality, which 'with its divisiveness and unceasing production of resentment, is clearly inimical to any reasonably healthy democratic development'.[29]

City in revolt

Ci's warnings about the need for realism in dealing with the CCP are most pointed—and poignant—when it comes to the fate of Hong Kong, where he has taught successive generations of students since the 1990s. Ci offered a trenchant diagnosis of Occupy Central, the Hong Kong democracy movement of 2014–15, whose driving passion, he argued, was not so much the desire for a representative political system *per se* but rather a longstanding identity of 'apartness and superiority' with regard to China. Born in part from the city's century-long evolution as a British colony, the contrast was heightened by Hong Kong's relative affluence and cosmopolitanism during the Cold War years, when Mao's China was

---

[27] DC, pp. 182, 165, 186.
[28] DC, p. 42.
[29] DC, pp. 208, 274.

'red and poor'. Yet this identity—based on 'a hierarchically and largely antagonistically conceived apartness from China'—was fragile and could only be maintained without stridency when Hong Kong's superiority was implicitly acknowledged by Beijing, as in the years after the city's return to the PRC's sovereignty in 1997, when 'China was busy becoming more like Hong Kong.' China's rise posed a problem for Hong Kong's sense of superior apartness, as the mainland population grew 'ever more capitalist, consumerist and fun-loving', even if—beyond the first-tier cities and the ranks of the well-to-do—it was 'less well-trained in middle-class sophistication and orderliness' than Hong Kongers claimed to be. For younger generations in Hong Kong, 'China is not cool', Ci notes; Beijing had yet to turn its 'hard power' into the capacity to win admiration and allegiance.[30]

The desire for apartness from China gave the Occupy Central movement the moral fervour and emotional cohesion of a national-liberation struggle, Ci argues; but this all-consuming defence of Hong Kong identity also crowded out other concerns, including social justice. Unlike its American namesake, Occupy Wall Street, the Hong Kong movement never targeted capitalism or called for Polanyi-style democracy with social protections; it hoped to ally with local tycoons against Beijing. Yet Ci is convinced that the movement's energy stemmed in part from pent-up frustration at the city's 'scandalous level of inequality' and the worsening prospects for its youth, in step with the advanced-capitalist world. Ci urged the students to rethink the substance of Hong Kong's apartness—to redefine it as less zero-sum, less hostile, more composed. A 'belligerent insistence on radical apartness' would be bound to provoke an overreaction from China. It was plain that Beijing would never allow the city to secede after its internationally recognized return to Chinese sovereignty in 1997, the fruit of a hundred-year wait. What the protesters called 'genuine democracy'—electing an anti-Beijing Chief Executive—was never on the cards. Hong Kong needed a political leadership that was neither a vassal of Beijing nor implacably opposed to it, with the integrity to disagree where necessary, within the bounds of the Basic Law. But Beijing also needed to listen to Hong Kong. 'Excessive self-righteousness' on both sides would only reinforce the vicious circle—driving Hong Kong's struggle to truly explosive proportions, or tempting Beijing to crush its desire for apartness by stamping out the

---

[30] DC, pp. 338–9, 334–5.

very basis for it, eliminating all that was different about Hong Kong. For four years before the final crackdown in 2020, Ci pleaded with the students to rewrite Kant's motto for the Enlightenment—not, 'Think freely, but obey', but 'Think freely, but exercise political restraint.'[31]

Yet if *Democracy in China*'s tactical prescriptions emphasized restraint, its diagnosis of the regime pulled no punches. Although the CCP showed no signs of abandoning its talk of socialism, its track record in recent decades was rather that of 'a massive apparatus for private appropriation', not just by corruption but through the perfectly legal entitlements enjoyed by higher officials and their families, allowing them to live 'as a species apart':

> What are [the Party's] socialist credentials anyway, other than its organizational continuity with Mao's CCP? Is there indeed still a communist party to speak of, given the inextricable links of the higher levels of its personnel and their relatives to the most powerful domestic capital and capitalists, and given the way it has been treating working people in terms of welfare provision, factor income distribution and protection against the worst ravages of capitalist exploitation?[32]

Nevertheless, it could not be concluded that the Party leadership was incapable of steering China onto another course, if its own legitimacy might be stabilized and strengthened in the process. In Ci's periodization, Jiang Zemin's rule in the 1990s had left an ambiguous legacy of 'political liberalization and moral anarchy', in almost equal measure. Under his successor Hu Jintao, the central political leadership (as distinct from state capacity) was at its weakest ever, 'neither loved nor feared', despite the return of repression in Hu's last years. Xi's leadership was definitely more feared, not least inside the Party, though more loved by some as well, at least in the earlier phases of his rule. (While the anti-corruption campaign had positive effects for a number of years, the reintroduction of the 'mass line' has never had much credibility.) Xi

---

[31] DC, pp. 340–1, 357, 355, 350, 362, 359, 368. An earlier version of the argument in *Democracy in China*'s chapter on Hong Kong was presented at a graduate conference at the University of Hong Kong in March 2016, under the title, 'Democracy in Hong Kong'. The talk was well attended by students active in the democracy movement, but many were left disappointed by Ci's call for political restraint and for advancing change instead at the social and cultural level, captured in what he called 'a democratic way of doing things'.

[32] DC, pp. 299–300.

had shown that it was still possible for an authoritative central leadership 'to turn Party and country in a new direction, good or bad'. Xi's choices could be crucial, Ci writes. Yet, 'Objectively speaking, Xi is an extraordinary leader and his is an extraordinary era'—extraordinary in the sense that contradictions which would normally produce 'an irresistible momentum towards fundamental change' were being effectively kept in check. However, there was no reason to believe that he would be followed by an equally extraordinary successor; things were likely to resume a more ordinary course in post-Xi China.[33]

The final section of *Democracy in China* turns to the international situation. On the world stage, Ci notes, China's rise appears lopsided: its economic growth and geopolitical clout have not been matched by a corresponding expansion in international legitimacy and respect. In part this is because the 'global political value space' as currently constituted makes democracy, however defined—Ci points elsewhere to the good standing of the *de facto* one-party system in Japan—a central condition for international legitimacy. China's geopolitical headaches largely spring from this 'lopsidedness', he argues, not least when it comes to 'domestic issues in which foreign powers happen to take a special political or geopolitical interest': intractable separatist tendencies in Tibet, Xinjiang, Hong Kong and Taiwan have a direct relation to the Chinese state's perceived lack of legitimacy, 'allowing the internal separatists and their external supporters and sympathizers to take the high moral ground'—and thereby 'subtly weakening' whatever sovereignty claims the state has against separatist challenges.[34]

Yet it would be wrong—indeed, undemocratic—for China to democratize purely at the behest of outside powers. A country's citizens remain the best judges of which political system is most 'fitting'. The external pressure is due in part to the 'political-system hostility' of liberal-democratic states, combining residual Cold War values with normative prescriptions, in a policy of regime change that poses a lethal threat to the CCP—counterproductively, for it warrants a permanent state of emergency and more repressive policies. Deploring such political-system hostility towards China as 'misguided' and 'unbecoming', Ci argues that

---

[33] DC, pp. 280–81, 300–301, 376.
[34] DC, pp. 311–13.

the most salutary and potent means of spurring the PRC's passage to democracy is not moralizing exhortation but 'positive example'. For the genuine egalitarian and democrat, Ci writes, maintaining the conditions for democracy within capitalism must involve a ceaseless struggle: there is no room for the complacent 'other-directed righteousness' that fuels political-system hostility. Democratic mechanisms may degenerate into 'little more than an ideological cover' for a distinctively capitalist form of imperium-dominium. 'It would be a double travesty if such an eviscerated democracy, instead of working to refill itself with democratic substance, turns around to channel what remains of its moral energy into political-system hostility against competitors who happen to be non-democratic.'[35]

Ci concludes on a note of trepidation. The Chinese leadership is understandably absorbed in the economic and international challenges of the moment, making statesmanlike foresight a luxury. It will be 'prohibitively difficult' for the CCP to give up its habit of taking no one's counsel but its own. How likely is Xi to be willing and able to prepare the way for greater popular agency, before he leaves the political stage? Yet Ci cannot but hope that this will prove wrong. If China's rise can continue without a paralysing crisis, the temptation to move towards democracy for the sake of international legitimacy and to stabilize the system could grow stronger. On the other hand, if a more powerful China is confronted with democracy's further decline, especially—through wars, imperial overreach, a new Gilded Age—in America itself, then all bets would be off.[36]

2. CONSIDERATIONS

By any measure, Ci's is a remarkable body of work, with few contemporary comparators, East or West—although, in their different ways, both Habermas and Bourdieu might come to mind. Within China, somewhat younger scholars such as Liu Qing (b. 1963), who teaches politics at ECNU, Shanghai, or Yao Yang (b. 1964), a political economist at Peking University, have covered some of the same ground, though neither is as

---

[35] DC, pp. 323, 315–7, 331–2, 324–5.
[36] DC, pp. 377–9.

philosophically minded nor as politically outspoken as Ci.[37] At the same time, Ci's profile remains relatively low in China; his Baidu page—an equivalent to Wikipedia—is largely in English, and he does not have an entry on Aisixiang, the website that republishes a great deal of work by PRC scholars. His books have been discussed in Anglophone scholarly journals and *Democracy in China* was the subject of a critical symposium in *Dao*, the Hong Kong-based international journal of comparative philosophy, in July 2022. Yet this may be the first attempt at a critical appreciation of his oeuvre as a whole.

Intellectually, the approach and style that Ci has honed since the 1990s represent a distinctive synthesis of tendencies and sources. Just as he is even-handed in his political criticisms of both East and West, he appears equally fluent in each tradition of political philosophy, on which he draws freely and eclectically to guide his reflections. His thought-world is perhaps most formed by Western philosophy, in particular its Continental strain: Nietzsche and Marx especially—the presiding influences on *Dialectic of the Chinese Revolution* and the only philosophers to whom Ci devoted entire courses during his teaching career—but also, though more sporadically, Spinoza and Norbert Elias, as well as Freud, Schopenhauer, Adorno and Tocqueville, among others.[38] In forging a 'philosopher's way of approaching history', Ci is sparing with empirical description: he is concerned with uncovering the logical conditions and structures of the Chinese experience, not documenting or explaining concrete historical developments (which are more 'often implied than presented in detail', as he has acknowledged).[39]

Conjugating cool reflection with deeply felt moral principles, interpretive abstraction with lived experience, Ci's lucid books, at once 'free and

---

[37] See for example Liu Qing, 'Liberalism in Contemporary China: Potential and Predicaments', tr. Matthew Galway and Lu Ha, 2013; and Yao Yang, 'The Dilemma of China's Democratization', tr. David Ownby, 2013 [2009]: both available online at *Reading the China Dream*; I'm grateful to David Ownby for indicating the relevance of these scholars' concerns to those of Ci Jiwei.
[38] Ci later added a course on Habermas, examining the complex relations between his thinking and that of Marx and Nietzsche. In *The Two Faces of Justice*, noting that he draws 'extensively on Western intellectual discourse', Ci writes that although he does not see himself as belonging to a 'particular school of philosophizing', he thinks that his way of thinking as a whole is more informed by Continental philosophy than by the analytic tradition, on which he also draws.
[39] Ci, *Dialectic of the Chinese Revolution*, p. 17.

precise', have a striking internal coherence and integrity, as though each must be accepted on its own terms, wholesale—aspiring to a form of intuitive recognition as much as rational persuasion.[40] At the same time, as a self-described 'principled realist', Ci combines analytic clarity and pragmatism with reformist urgency. His writing, though philosophical and abstracted, is conceived as an attempt to intervene in, as well as to interpret, the situation he diagnoses. Yet his prescriptions, he insists, are circumscribed by what is necessary, 'prudent' and possible given local conditions.

Modes of agency

How should we begin to characterize Ci's thematics? One concept that offers a guiding thread through his thinking is that of agency. The theme played a substantial role in *Dialectic of the Chinese Revolution*, albeit there mostly in the shape of the will to power, forced to express itself 'in the will to nothingness', setting 'a paradisiac future of communism, rationally known to be beyond human reach, above a present doomed forever to be imperfect.'[41] Ci developed the concept further in a 2013 paper theorizing poverty.[42] Human agency then became the explicit organizing concept of *Moral China*, making this book a pivotal point in the evolving framework of the trilogy. As we have seen, he here differentiated agency-through-identification from agency-through-freedom, identified with the incomplete transition from the dynastic to juridical state. What distinguishes these modes of agency, and the respective moral cultures that facilitate them? First, the degree to which the moral culture permits citizens to form an independent relationship to 'the good'—to think for themselves, rather than follow a moral exemplar (sage rulers, Mao, Xi)—or, as Ci would put it in *Democracy in China*, their capacity to act on the basis of individual responsibility. The normative core of Ci's view, if one

---

[40] 'Free and precise' are the terms Ci uses in *Moral China* to describe his freewheeling use of Freud: 'I find his way of thinking and some of his ideas suggestive in a way that allows me to be free and precise at the same time—free with regard to Freud as a source of insights and precise in formulating my own hypotheses'. The passage is striking for Ci's claim that it is immaterial to the validity of his hypotheses whether Freud's ideas are correct or not, whether his own understanding of them is accurate or not, and whether his uses of those ideas are 'appropriate' or not: p. 109.

[41] Ci, *Dialectic of the Chinese Revolution*, p. 195.

[42] Ci, 'Agency and Other Stakes of Poverty', *Journal of Political Philosophy*, vol. 21, 2013.

could call it that, resides in his conviction that the superiority of a properly juridical state to a dynastic one, and therefore of the citizen to the
subject, is to be found, first and foremost, in improved forms of agency.[43]

Ci understands freedom as the room for manoeuvre required for the
meaningful exercise of human agency under modern conditions. If
the two categories, agency and freedom, have something transhistori-
cal about them, Ci emphasizes that we are speaking about modern
times and modern freedoms (quoting Benjamin Constant). This turns
freedom from a metaphysical principle into a sociohistorical one: a condition required by agents in modern capitalist societies. It also leaves the
content of freedom and agency open, which matters for Ci's purposes.
The question of freedom appears as the central motivating thought
in *Democracy in China*, from which the subsequent prudential argument for democracy can be taken to derive. Indeed, the argument for
democracy may almost appear secondary—as a logical upshot of the
question of freedom. Why else would Ci quote at length Spinoza's argument for freedom of thought as a natural property of human beings in
a footnote to the discussion of freedom in the chapter on 'democratic
preparation'? In this context, freedom matters, first and foremost, as an
essential condition for the new moral subjectivity required by changed
social conditions, and is necessary too for the robust civil society that
would be capable of providing an independent source of social and
political stability.

Here again, Bourdieu's enigmatic pointers for thinking against the grain
of the state may illuminate Ci's singular perspective. *Moral China*'s med-
itations upon freedom and equality—and the pervasive predispositions
towards them that Ci sees in contemporary Chinese society, at least with
regard to opportunity, non-discrimination and political rights—seem to
have carried him closer to Tocqueville, for whom freedom and equality
represent a dialectic value pair (*people are free because they are equal, and
equal because they are free*). In Bourdieu's terms, theorizing freedom in the
way Ci does is neither 'state thinking' nor 'thought produced by society',
since the *de facto* freedoms everyone is in principle encouraged to enjoy
as members of the 'moderately prosperous' (*xiaokang*) society are not
understood in terms of freedom as a value. In other words, the concepts
of freedom and equality—concepts which CCP discourse acknowledges,

---

[43] For all their shared concern with the state, it is their very different conceptions of
human agency that set Ci and Bourdieu apart.

at least at face value, as 'core values of socialism'—may afford Ci a larger space for theorizing than could be found in the shadow of liberal justice. It is this possibility that informs Ci's repeated focus on what he calls, in a chapter title of *Moral China*, 'Freedom's Unfinished Task'.

Justice, too, for Ci, requires the reciprocity of popular agency—'the socialization of justice'—even as the state remains 'its sovereign guardian'. Xi Jinping's ongoing anti-corruption campaign might be a case in point here: while it indicates a real determination to correct decades of state failure in safeguarding even the semblance of reciprocity, it also reveals China's arduous road ahead in (re)socializing a sense of justice, for which a degree of trust in the state is a structural requirement. The successful management of justice for its citizens is one criterion of the juridical state's legitimacy, a measure of its capacity to maintain lasting social cohesion. Where it fails to inspire people's willingness to follow norms, a moral crisis is set in motion. At the onset of such a crisis, intellectual incoherence also emerges as a concomitant symptom. What the state does, what it says it does, and how it inspires people to think and act, tend to fall into disarray.

As one moves from *Dialectic* to *Moral China* to *Democracy in China*, the overcoming of the crisis of the body, not through utopia but through the market, comes at the price of moral subjectivity, with the lack of an effective new ideological order.[44] In Ci's view, this has produced an asymmetry between the state's capacity to rule by force and its inability to lead through moral approval. What makes the Chinese state an 'almost unthinkable' object today, therefore, is not simply that it circumscribes the terms with which we can think it—that would be a sign of its successful universalism—but rather that the terms the state continues to use have become floating signifiers without clear objects of identity. At stake here is what Bourdieu would call 'doxic comprehension'—the ability to take the state for granted, to grasp it as a natural thing.

When China commentators talk of 'nominal' Marxism or a 'nominally' Communist Party, they suggest that the name has survived the death of

---

[44] It is notable that there are no direct references to Confucianism, capitalism or liberalism in the Party's most recent 'historical resolution', entitled *Resolution of the Central Committee of the Communist Party of China on the Major Achievements and Historical Experience of the Party over the Past Century*, released to mark the CCP's centenary in October 2021. This document is the third of its kind, following Mao's in 1945 and Deng's in 1981–82.

its meaning and that the Party bears only a terminological semblance to its founding principles. Ci, for his part, does not take the CCP to task in terms of how *communist* it really is. He, too, accepts the 'nominal' reality of its name, yet it is precisely its name that confers real and singular power, underwriting its title to rule. Why else would all the Party's grand political goals be framed in temporal reference to the revolution—1921, 1949, 2021, 2049? And why else cast even the management of the pandemic in terms of Mao's concept of people's war (*renmin zhanzheng*), dating back to 1927? As a political and moral resource, the term is designed as a reminder of the CCP's historic claim to legitimacy through exceptional victorious struggle. To be sure, the Party has taken the phrase out of its old context, without having to worry that any Chinese speaker would interpret the invocation of *renmin zhanzheng* as a call for class war. Yet it is symptomatic that phraseologies float around at will, with people in official contexts 'going through linguistic motions'. This lack of intellectual coherence stymies the state's grand ambition of establishing a universality equal in coherence to that of its adversary across the Pacific. What stands in the way can be captured in the Confucian principle of *zhengming* or 'rectification of names', according to which anything real and lasting in the political sphere can only be accomplished once names and language are in accord with truth.[45]

Xi and after

Critics of *Democracy in China* largely converge in charging Ci with excessive optimism about the plausibility of the CCP undertaking reforms that would grant the populace greater political freedom and agency—especially of a kind that might bring an end to its rule.[46] In his reply to critics, published in *Dao*, Ci reiterated the point that he does not claim that democratization led by an enlightened CCP is likely; what he claims is that the Chinese state will face the prospect of '*either* democratiza-

---

[45] Ci invokes the principle of *zhengming* in DC, pp. 108 and 390, n. 10.

[46] See Joseph Chan, 'Is Democracy Coming to Knock on China's Door? Reply to Jiwei Ci's *Democracy in China*', *Dao*, July 2022; Sungmoon Kim, 'Tocqueville between America and China and Democracy', *Dao*, July 2022; Ci's reply to both, 'Democracy in China: Reply to My Critics', *Dao*, July 2022; Biao Teng, 'Is China Ready for Democracy?', *Law & Liberty*, 22 September 2020; Yu-Wen Chen, 'An Unconventional but Prudent Proposal for China's Democratization', *European Political Sciences*, vol. 20, June 2022; Chi Kwok, '(Un)realistic Utopia: Rethinking Political Legitimacy, Democracy and Resistance in China', *Contemporary Political Theory*, vol. 20, 2021.

tion *or* crisis'. For Ci, as we have seen, mounting repression cannot be a long-term solution; on the contrary, it merely indicates the growing scale of discontent that needs to be repressed. Ci has addressed these points repeatedly and none of his critics has so far managed to explain why heightened repression is necessary in the first place, or why asking to live without it is not an unreasonable demand. His reviewers may cite the vastly enhanced high-tech capacities of the Chinese state, from its omniscient social-credit system to its DNA collection, biometric tags and facial-recognition programmes; but Ci would not disagree with them about the scope of its 'deterrence effect'.[47]

Indeed, the CCP may have switched, as Eric Hobsbawm observed of communist states more generally, from an epoch powered by the 'engine of revolution' to one driven by the 'engine of conservation'.[48] Xi Jinping's invocation of the China Dream (*zhongguo meng*), whose substance is 'the great rejuvenation of the Chinese nation', may be read as just such a conservation exercise. It is not a dream informed by any socialist conception of 'the good' nor any Marxian project of emancipation. In the terminology of Yang Guangbin, a political scientist and Marxism expert close to the regime, the Chinese party-state has moved from 'seeking change' (*qiubian*) to 'seeking order' (*qiuzhi*).[49] This paradigm shift to *zhi*, or order, is twofold: a return to the 2,000-year-old civilizational history of China which shows that the Chinese are, according to Yang, 'inherently governance-minded', with the government 'putting the people first' (*renmin zhishang*), a principle derived from the tradition of the Legalist-Confucian state. Yang calls this arrangement 'Confucian outside and Legalist inside', arguing that it is deeply rooted in the Chinese 'cultural gene'. The historical weight of *zhi* is captured in the term *zhizhi* or, as Yang translates it elsewhere, 'making the country politically stable and peaceful'.[50]

---

[47] DC, p. 42.

[48] Eric Hobsbawm, *The Age of Extremes. The Short Twentieth Century: 1914–1991*, London 1995, p. 368.

[49] In English, see Yang Guangbin, 'The Paradigm Shift of Political Science from Being "Change-oriented" to "Governance-oriented": A Perspective on History of Political Science', *Chinese Political Science Review*, no. 6, 2021, pp. 506–45; the original article was published in Chinese in 2018. Yang Guangbin is a member of the Foreign Affairs Committee of the Chinese People's Political Consultative Conference (CPPCC), Dean of the School of International Studies at Renmin University of China and Chief Expert of the CPC's Marxist Project.

[50] See the interview summary by Li Chun, 'Yang Guangbin: Why Is Modernization of State Governance Never Equal to Westernization?', *ECNS Wire*, 6 December 2021.

The CCP continues to sell itself, not as the vanguard in the global strug-gle against capitalism, but as the true representative—the 'real heroes', in Mao's phrase—of the masses, whose interests entirely converge with its own. In 2021, on the occasion of the Party's centenary, Xi Jinping himself asserted its representational superiority, on the grounds that it had 'no special interests of its own'—'it has never represented any individual interest group, power group or privileged stratum.'[51] Whether that is true or not is an empirical matter; but that it needed to be claimed goes to the heart of things, for in the absence of elections some other credible basis for representation has to be found. For some theorists, the solution lies in the Maoist tradition of the 'mass line' (*qunzhong luxian*)—consulting the masses, interpreting their will, implementing policies in their interests.[52] Yet as the political philosopher Lin Chun put it, Xi's recent attempt to resurrect the concept 'sounded hollow'—this was a different Party to Mao's, and the alienation of officials from 'the masses' was an everyday experience: 'families of the "red aristoc-racy" and the new elites have enriched themselves at an unprecedented speed and scale by devouring state resources and colluding with private (domestic and foreign) capital.'[53]

'Fairness' as a fix?

Critics of Ci's realist hope-against-hope for the self-reform of the state also need to deal with his argument that China's new 'equality of condi-tions', brought about by Maoist egalitarianism and Dengist economic liberalization, will lead to pressure for political liberalization—a view shared by many policymakers in the West, between roughly 1992 and 2012, although they would deny Mao any credit. A standard criticism is that 'equality of conditions' is belied by China's soaring *inequality* of incomes; but, as we have seen, Ci's case allows for this. A more seri-ous objection might be that, Xi's denials notwithstanding, the CCP has

---

[51] In English, see 'Full Text of Xi Jinping's Speech on the CCP's 100th Anniversary', *Nikkei Asia*, 1 July 2021.
[52] The CCP's official position on representation has for the past twenty years been summed up in the concept of the Three Represents. Proponents of a revivified 'mass line' include Daniel Bell and Wang Pei, *Just Hierarchy: Why Social Hierarchies Matter in China and the Rest of the World*, Princeton 2020; Tongdong Bai, *Against Political Equality: The Confucian Case*, Princeton 2020.
[53] Lin Chun, 'Mass Line', in Christian Sorace, Ivan Frenceschini and Nicholas Loubere, eds, *Afterlives of Chinese Communism*, London and New York 2019, p. 125.

acquired proto-class interests that would prevent it from conceding the Polanyian social protections against the market that Ci's 'preparations for democracy' require. Conceptually, Ci's work allows for such a pushback by the CCP. His prudential argument for democracy on the basis of social 'fittingness' draws upon the mechanism of the spillover effect that Jon Elster had detected in Tocqueville.[54] This posits that a pattern of behaviour in one sphere of life may be expected to spill over into others; here, consumer freedoms rippling into the political sphere. But the state may also attempt to block the spillover by using what Elster called the compensation effect. For Ci, as we have seen, an example would be what happened in the wake of 4 June 1989, when the Chinese state satisfied the hedonistic demands underlying the democracy movement with ever-increasing abundance, sufficient to block the political aspirations of the time. Linked to the strategy of hedonistic compensation—for Ci, always a strategy of buying time—is Elster's 'crowding-out effect', which diverts energies devoted to one end towards another; in Ci's adaptation, desire for democracy was diverted into desire for more money (the underlying Nietzschean idea is that people's energy is as flexible as it is limited).

The proliferation of the term 'fairness' (*gongping*), which has permeated both official parlance and everyday speech in recent years, might thus be read as a last discursive resort—an attempt to buy time by promoting a value which, while it does not make any direct demand, can function as a close enough proxy for one to delay the spillover effect. In Xi Jinping's *The Governance of China*, a much-reissued collection of his speeches, 'fairness' appears no fewer than eighty times.[55] The importance of the idea, unthinkable and unnecessary under Mao, is an index of the ideological outlook of the contemporary CCP. Neither a traditional value nor a foundational Marxist-Leninist principle, fairness became the perfect normative fit for the party-state and for a society subject to free-market laws. Free-market fairness, its advocates must be aware, is never really fair, just as the market is never really free. But the useful amorphousness of the term appears to satisfy the political needs of the moment.

---

[54] Jon Elster, *Alexis de Tocqueville, the First Social Scientist*, Cambridge 2009, esp. Chapter One; the notion of a neofunctionalist spillover mechanism had been discussed by Ernst Haas in *The Uniting of Europe* (1958).
[55] While it should be noted that 'democracy', 'equality' and 'freedom' also appear dozens of times in Xi's *Governance of China* and in official CCP discourse, these terms that also appear in Marx, whereas 'fairness' does not.

The rise of fairness goes hand in hand with the promotion of 'common prosperity' (*gongtong fuyu*), whose positive meaning has been left carefully vague. Beijing's policy advisers have made clear that 'common prosperity' is not about building an egalitarian or welfare state, nor 'robbing the rich to help the poor'; the point is rather to bake 'a bigger and better cake'.[56] Yet the quasi-Rawlsian emphasis on fairness may eventually prove both a blessing and a curse. While 'fairness' can assign positive value to competitive inequalities—if they can be shown to be 'fair', which they almost always can—it might also open a Pandora's box of struggles for real equality. China's fast-growing private sector now accounts for almost 90 per cent of urban employment (up from 18 per cent in the mid-1990s), while the gig-economy is projected to double its current work force of 200 million—a quarter of China's entire labour force—to 400 million workers by 2036. How the regime governs this informal sphere of the labouring masses, mostly made up of migrant workers who enjoy neither fairness nor freedom, could prove its Achilles heel.

Ci's prudential case for democratic reform is motivated by his sense that the coming crisis will be contained only at unbearable cost. His (slender) hope that the Party will understand that such reform is in its own interest must wrestle with the reality that the CCP still enjoys an impregnable monopoly of physical violence. Ci's case builds on the sobering lessons learned from China's last serious push for democracy in 1989, when students, workers and intellectuals failed in their efforts to orient protest and rhetoric towards any unified political outcome. By contrast, the intransigent elderly elite, with its hold over the military, united under Chen Yun's slogan: 'We the veteran comrades must step forward boldly'—'we must never make concessions.'[57]

That the Party once possessed democratic senses of its own is evident from its history. China's pre-war tradition of democratic discourse, from which the CCP's own founding members had once emerged as the radicals prizing revolution over reform, has no lack of resources in the writings of Liang Qichao, Hu Shi, Zhang Dongsun, Zhang Junmai and others. The urgency of Ci's arguments for reform, palpable on every page of his books, is not, however, a reliable measure of the degree

---

[56] 'China's Common Prosperity Boon to World', Xinhua News, 21 December 2021.
[57] Quoted in Merle Goldman, *Sowing the Seeds of Democracy in China: Political Reform in the Deng Xiaoping Era*, Cambridge 1994, p. 327.

to which the Party may actually be willing to change itself.[58] Failing that, China's democratic imaginary has been transformed from a head without a body, a century ago, to a body—the moderately prosperous society—without a head. How well, how soon and in what way the pressure for democracy may yet give rise to a decisive phase of regime transformation remains a matter of political speculation. Ci places the burden of responsibility for change primarily on the shoulders of the ruling elite; he thereby also directs the discussion away from apolitical moral righteousness toward hard questions of political possibility under China's current conditions.

Beginning in *Dialectic of the Chinese Revolution* and continuing with *Moral China*, Ci diagnosed a psychological-moral crisis with identifiable roots in social mismanagement and political misjudgement, understood as the historical movement from utopianism to nihilism and hedonism. With *Democracy in China*, Ci has come to think China's crisis from the other side, perhaps manifesting the kind of deterministic prognosis, or *Zwangsprognose*, that Koselleck identified in French revolutionary philosophies of history, beginning with the Abbé de Raynal.[59] To the degree that there is an air of determinism in Ci's late thought, it is not one of moralizing utopianism, the dangers and failures of which had been laid bare in *Dialectic*, but one of political consonance and the logic of human agency, pulling Chinese society in the direction of freedom and equality. But to what end, one might ask, given that these proclaimed values have more often than not turned out to be disguises for their very opposite? Ci's answer must be: for a better totality. This new totality would add public-political design to what has already come about at the level of ordinary life. It would therefore achieve much greater ideological potency than the current situation has to offer, or can be expected to offer, if China's route—real and imaginary—to a superior political arrangement is blocked by design, by misadventure, or by another disastrous combination of the two.

---

[58] An old political wisdom from John Dunn, *The Politics of Socialism: An Essay in Political Theory*, Cambridge 1984, p. 21.
[59] Reinhart Koselleck, *Kritik und Krise, Eine Studie zur Pathogenese der bürgerlichen Welt*, Frankfurt 1976, pp. 146–7.

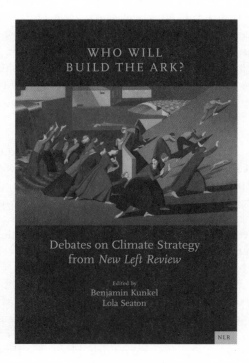

NIC JOHNSON

TIMES OF INTEREST

Longue-Durée Rates and Capitalist Stabilization

O NE OF THE many transformations that capitalism has brought
about is in our subjective experience of time. To our ancestors,
time was measured in the steady cyclical rhythms of agrarian
society, punctuated by occasional catastrophes like war, famine or plague. We moderns experience it as progressive and open-ended;
dependent on the market and its capricious outcomes, we have to wager
on a radically uncertain future. As individuals, this is said to make us
both anxious and optimistic. Over the last generation, however, capitalism has settled into a deep stagnation that has drained optimism from
large swathes of our societies. Signs of it are all around—from median
incomes and productivity growth to the recycling of Marvel movies.[1]
Mainstream economists like Robert Gordon, Thomas Piketty and Larry
Summers have been sounding the tocsin about capitalism's lack of dynamism for some time now. What has gone wrong?

A series of objective relations that manage time under capitalism might
plausibly explain our current malaise. The rate of profit on productive
capital has received the lion's share of attention on the left, perhaps second only to the length of the working day. But another relation is just as
important: the rate of interest. Unlike profits, whose tendency to decline
is debatable—bogged down in difficult arguments about how to calculate
it and largely unobservable outside the recent advanced world—interest
rates can be read directly off the historical record and, as we shall see,
their long-run tendency to fall is incontestable. Interest rates are also
central to the way that modern states manage the rhythms of their mac-
roeconomies. Over the course of the business cycle, central banks adjust
interest rates to stabilize aggregate demand. Faced with recession,

governments cut rates to revive private investment; confronted with inflation, governments hike rates to cut it off. Our collective economic ups and downs are closely linked to the rate of interest.[2]

I. DOWN TO ZERO

Recent near-zero interest-rate policies (ZIRPs) are both an index and a cause of capitalism's contradictory political condition today. In a typical postwar recession, the Fed lowered short-term rates by just over 5 percentage points. But after the global financial crisis those rates were stuck near zero and could not go lower, blunting their stabilizing force. Without this tool to fight recession, capitalism muddled through the stagnant 2010s and survived the coronavirus shutdowns only with the help of massive fiscal and monetary stimulus. Until March 2022, the Fed had its policy rate pinned to the floor at zero yet again, and though it has risen over the last eighteen months, it seems unlikely that today's higher rates will last; current models have them trending down again in 2024 and 2025. But it is not just the short rate that has recently been malfunctioning perilously close to zero: ten-year US Treasuries tanked to barely 0.54 per cent in 2020. Other parts of the world have experienced even more advanced states of decline, with negative rates out to even longer maturities. Japan is an especially harrowing case: its short-term bills have been stuck at the zero-lower bound on and off since the 1990s, its ten-year bond playing footsie with the zero-lower bound since 2016.

---

[1] The *locus classicus* on the advent of capitalist time is Edward Thompson, 'Time, Work-Discipline and Industrial Capitalism', *Past & Present*, no. 38, December 1967. In the late 1970s, the percentage of Top-20 movies by revenue that were either prequels, sequels, spinoffs, remakes or reboots was below 25 per cent; it is over 75 per cent today.

[2] A note on terminology: 'nominal' rates are the headline rates on debt; 'real' rates are constructed by subtracting inflation from the nominal rate. Unless otherwise specified, 'interest rate' in this essay refers to a nominal rate on sovereign debt. Nominal rates have an effective lower bound because cash has a nominal return of zero, so it is possible to avoid a negative return on investment by simply holding cash. Real rates can theoretically decline as far as inflation can rise. Negative nominal rates are possible—and prominent over the last decade—despite arbitrage with the zero per cent returns on cash ostensibly putting a floor beneath them, because the storage costs of cash turn out to be higher than those of government debt. The costs of physically warehousing the paper involved means that rates can become slightly negative, but there is an 'effective lower bound' somewhere just below zero.

Interest rate management has less room to perform its assigned stabilization tasks in the face of recession than in previous eras.

The interest-rate declines after 2008 and 2020 were justified as a response to the business cycle, just as the current hikes are justified as a response to inflation. But it is the initial, already-low position of interest rates prior to the global crises that must be explained, since across these cycles there has been an unambiguous secular decline. Indeed, American interest rates were falling across the maturity spectrum for nearly two generations (Figure 1, below and overleaf).

FIGURE 1: *US Nominal Interest Rates, Selected Maturities, 1985–2023*

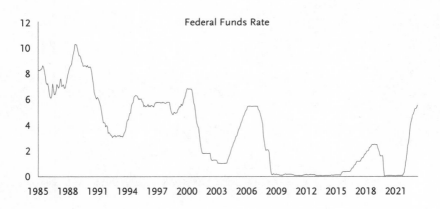

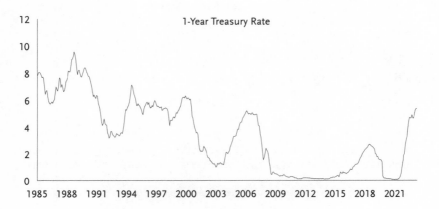

FIGURE I: *US Nominal Interest Rates, Selected Maturities, 1985–2023*

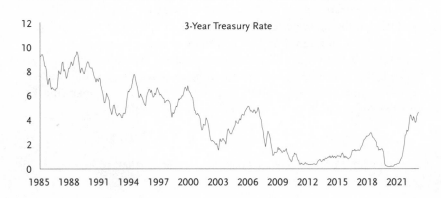

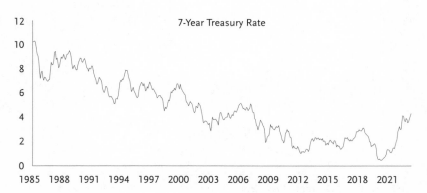

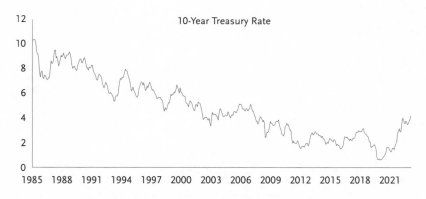

Source: St. Louis Federal Reserve Economic Data.

FIGURE 2: *Global Real Interest Rates, 1311–2018*

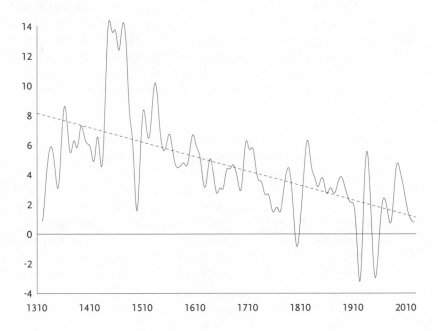

Source: Paul Schmelzing, 'Eight Centuries of Global Real Interest Rates, R-G and the "Suprasecular" Decline, 1311–2018'. The Bank of England's data has been passed through a Hodrick-Prescott filter, to remove low-frequency fluctuations, and a linear time trend added.

To understand our current malaise, however, a longer time horizon is needed. A fascinating recent dataset constructed by Paul Schmelzing at the Bank of England, which traces real interest rates from the early 14th century, shows a slow downward trend persisting over 700 years—through different tax regimes, monetary policies, social systems, cultural revolutions and international contexts (Figure 2, above).[3] It is impossible to explain this finding by reference to any concurrent policy change or

[3] Paul Schmelzing, 'Eight Centuries of Global Real Interest Rates, R-G and the "Suprasecular" Decline, 1311–2018', Bank of England Staff Working Paper, no. 845, 3 January 2020; the BoE dataset has nominal sovereign interest rates dating back to 1273 and real interest rates dating from 1311.

a complex of policy choices; the trend is too long and too persistent.[4] Sophisticated statistical tests looking for breaks or changes in trend can find only two: the devastating Black Death of 1346–53, the plague estimated to have killed over 30 per cent of the European population, and the sovereign defaults by France, Spain and the Netherlands in 1557.[5] The downward trend has worked slowly but consistently since the birth of public debt in the high middle ages. It may therefore be rooted in the structural dynamics of the expanding capitalist world-system itself—which means that the problems posed by today's zero-lower bounds are unlikely to be temporary.

Understanding the causes of this long-term trend requires critical engagement with recent scholarship on finance and its history. Because the interest rate does a substantial amount of work in regulating the dynamics of capitalism, there are also many processes operating on different time scales at work in its determination. Although the chronicle of interest rates comes down to us as a series in empty, homogeneous time, it is possible to decompose the different frequencies at which it fluctuates to analyse them separately.[6] In the following, I will proceed from the longest time scale necessary for understanding today's low

---

[4] This presents us with something of a puzzle, since the evidence points to a strong role for monetary authorities in interest-rate determination: the vast majority of price changes in bond markets happen within a 72-hour window of monetary-policy announcements (see Sebastian Hillenbrand, 'The Fed and the Secular Decline in Interest Rates', Working Paper, January 2022). While monetary authorities today have overwhelming power to determine liquidity conditions in financial markets, and hence the overall level of interest rates, they have not *always* had this power, nor consciously used it. And yet, the forces pushing rates down have been operating more or less continuously, pushing global real rates down at the same pace for centuries. But if modern monetary authorities can choose where to set policy rates, they do not do so *arbitrarily*; the question then becomes, what determines their choices? If it is the same forces that have been operating for centuries, the puzzle is resolved: liquidity's central planners are merely the medium through which deeper determinations operate.

[5] Schmelzing and colleagues conducted a series of econometric tests and robustness checks to demonstrate that the global long-run rates are 'trend stationary': see Kenneth Rogoff, Barbara Rossi and Paul Schmelzing, 'Long-Run Trends in Long-Maturity Real Rates, 1311–2021', NBER Working Paper no. 30475, October 2022.

[6] Braudel, *On History*, trans. Sarah Matthews, Chicago 1980, Part 2: History and the Other Human Sciences; Reinhart Koselleck, *Futures Past: On the Semantics of Historical Time*, New York 2004, chapter 14.

rates—as it turns out, all 700 years of public debt's history—down to the shortest, the capitalist business cycle. The various timescales each overlay one another, giving the line on the chart an uneven and combined character, which nevertheless has a clear and rationally comprehensible directionality. This paper will discuss the birth, spread and consolidation of safe assets, before examining the major transformations that have operated to push rates down over the past century or so—and what they may mean for our political future. But first it may be helpful to set down some more general considerations about what it is that we are measuring and trying to theorize when we speak of interest rates.

2. BEDROCK OF CAPITAL

All economic actors need stores of value. Workers planning their retirement, corporations managing cash flow, banks posting collateral or central banks holding currency with which to stabilize forex markets—all need legal assets to transmit value through time.[7] The so-called 'safe rates of interest' determine how easily that's done—the higher the safe rates, the easier it is for individuals to transmit value to the future, shielded against erosion by inflation or default. Some assets—like the US government's debts—stand out for their low default risk, easy tradability and the fact that their value is relatively uncorrelated with other major risks, all of which make them useful for hedging. These assets are the benchmark unit against which others are valued; corporate securities, for example, are priced by adding a 'risk premium' over government debt with equivalent maturity.[8] Safe assets may also circulate as a medium of exchange, as was the case with bills of exchange in the early-modern period, or US Treasuries flying back and forth in global repo markets today. In short, when an asset is truly safe, it acts like money.

As one might expect, safety here is relative and constitutes a spectrum, along which we can find different kinds of monies and near-monies,

---

[7] Ricardo Caballero, Emmanuel Farhi and Pierre-Olivier Gourinchas, 'The Safe Assets Shortage Conundrum', *Journal of Economic Perspectives*, vol. 31, no. 3, Summer 2017, pp. 29–46; Jonathan Levy, 'Capital as Process and the History of Capitalism', *Business History Review*, vol. 91, no. 3, pp. 483–510.

[8] See Stephen Marglin, *Raising Keynes: A Twenty-first-century General Theory*, Cambridge MA 2021, chapters 11 and 12, for a theory of anchors and spreads.

issued by many different kinds of institutions.[9] From central banks and Treasury departments to crypto hedge funds and Third World dictators, many institutions *try* to issue safe assets. The difficulties lie in getting other people to accept them and delivering on the promise of safety. The ability to produce safe assets depends upon state capacity, constraints within the financial sector, the general level of development—and reputation. Thus, the actual issuance of safe assets has mostly been confined to actors close to states in the advanced-capitalist core. The rate of interest on that debt—the 'safe rate'—balances that supply of safe assets against the demand for them. It also serves as a reference rate for other kinds of investments: if a sovereign bond offers a safe 5 per cent, then building a factory is only worth it if the profits are expected to be substantially higher, to compensate for the risk involved.

Closely related to safety is liquidity. The meaning and role of 'liquidity' comes into sharper focus when what Hyman Minsky called the 'survival constraint' is taken into account. Every economic unit—individuals, households, firms, banks, governments—has inflows and outflows, payments made to them and payments they need to make. 'Survival' requires making those payments—whether to grocery stores, landlords, employees, creditors or military contractors.[10] This is the balance-sheet expression of what Marxists later called 'market dependence'. Failure to survive capitalism has different consequences for different actors, from starvation and homelessness to Chapter 12 bankruptcy, sovereign default to revolution. To avoid situations in which inflows are insufficient to match outflows, economic units need to acquire assets with which they can make direct payments (liquid cash) or which they can easily sell to acquire cash (market liquidity), or to line up access to credit so that they can issue new liabilities to acquire means of payment (funding liquidity). The liquidity of a balance sheet as a whole is its ability to 'meet the claims, of whatever kinds, that may be made' upon it.[11] Given the role of radical uncertainty under capitalism, liquidity is always a matter of convention and judgement, and thus self-referential loops.

[9] Perry Mehrling, 'Essential Hybridity: A Money View of FX', *Journal of Comparative Economics*, vol. 41, no. 2, 2013, pp. 355–63; Perry Mehrling, 'The Inherent Hierarchy of Money', in Armon Rezai, Lance Taylor, Thomas Michl, eds., *Social Fairness and Economics: Economic Essays in the Spirit of Duncan Foley*, Abingdon 2012.
[10] Perry Mehrling, 'The Vision of Hyman P. Minsky', *Journal of Economic Behavior & Organization*, vol. 39, 1999, pp. 129–58.
[11] John Hicks, 'Liquidity', *Economic Journal*, vol. 72, no. 288, 1962; see also Jean Tirole, 'Illiquidity and All Its Friends', *Journal of Economic Literature*, vol. 49, no. 2, June 2011.

US Treasury securities are liquid because, unlike more boutique capital assets, they are highly standardized and everyone in the world trades them, from Kansas farmers saving for retirement to communist central banks, making them easy to buy and sell quickly, in bulk, without moving their price.

What does liquidity have to do with interest rates? Assets that are relatively illiquid are relatively unattractive to investors, so they have to compensate by offering a higher yield if their issuers are to attract buyers. Consider the difference between holding $100 in cash versus buying a 10-year bond with a face value of $100 yielding a yearly return of $2. Why would anyone hold cash when the bond pays interest? The answer is liquidity: in a financial panic, in which payments must be made quickly, the cash will always work; the bond, however, will have to be sold to someone else willing to hold it. If held to maturity, the bond would eventually pay out $100+2*10. But that is ten years from now; if the cash is needed today, it might be necessary to accept a large capital loss on the value of bond holdings to make it through the crisis. It is that risk—that, in a pinch, the market value drops—which the forward-thinking investor has in mind when demanding the $2 yield, as compensation for holding the relatively illiquid asset.

The 'safe rate' helps to satisfy the preference for liquidity in the face of capitalist uncertainty, by putting a floor under economic actors' losses and uncertainties. When I put 40 per cent of my retirement fund into US government bonds and 60 per cent into stocks, I know the former will still be there in thirty years, and it is only on that basis that I am willing to gamble on corporations as well. Banks are more complicated but not essentially different. Without a safety net, most of us are unwilling to walk the tightrope. We must first satisfy our preference for liquidity before moving on to other projects. For the economy as a whole, the extent of safe assets allows economic agents to take the risks without which capitalism cannot function. The $32 trillion worth of US federal government debt forms the bedrock on which the rest of the global capital structure rests.[12]

---

[12] Christopher Carroll, 'Buffer-Stock Saving and the Life Cycle/Permanent Income Hypothesis', *Quarterly Journal of Economics*, vol. 112, no. 1, February 1997, pp. 1–55. It is a problem for global capitalism that states have generally produced imperfectly safe assets, and in such small portions: Germany ($2.1bn, AAA), Canada ($1.3bn, AA+), France ($2.4bn, AA-), UK ($2.6bn, AA-), China ($8.7bn, A+), Japan ($7.7bn, A), Italy ($2.3bn, BBB). Quantities from the Bank for International Settlements, ratings from Fitch.

It is at this point that the *longue durée* offers some purchase. Another study of the Bank of England datasets has constructed a remarkable time series by concatenating the terms offered to the most stable and secure sovereigns in the capitalist world-system since 1311: a synthetic series for 'Northern Italian' debt issued by the city-states (Venice, Genoa, Florence), followed by series for Spain, Holland, Britain, Germany and the US (the 'leading safe issuer series').[13] Maturities up to ten years were available, and there was not a single instance of bankruptcy on any of the debt included. To the extent that safe assets existed, these were it.

Notably, these issuers also represent the successive leading states in Giovanni Arrighi's *The Long Twentieth Century*. In Arrighi's account, after each phase of 'real' expansion comes to an end, an era of 'financial' expansion ensues, amid geopolitical chaos, as capitalists in the leading state liquidate their assets to prepare for the next hegemonic cycle. The state best able to reconfigure its institutions then absorbs the new investments, restarting real growth in the world-system on an expanded scale. The key institutional innovations were more liquid investment markets—bourses, central banking, limited liability, deposit banking— and a larger fiscal state and internal market, capable of sustaining a higher global floor for effective demand. For Arrighi, these issuers—the 15th-century Italian city-states, 16th-century Spain, 17th-century Holland, 19th-century Britain, the 20th-century US—did indeed represent the most advanced economies in their respective 'long centuries'.[14]

As registered above, the most striking feature of the Bank of England series is that these interest rates have a long-run tendency to fall. For the full 700-year sample, the short-term safe real rate falls on average by about 0.9 per cent per century. That might not seem like much; but projected forward from the high point of the 1400s, when the safe rate was nearly 9.1 per cent on average, it represents a very substantial decline. Importantly, unlike the 'global' real rate on sovereign debt—constructed by taking the average of Italy, UK, Holland, Germany, France, US, Spain

[13] Paul Schmelzing, 'Eight Centuries of the Risk-Free Rate: Bond Market Reversals from the Venetians to the "VaR shock"', Bank of England Staff Working Paper, no. 686, 20 October 2017.

[14] Giovanni Arrighi, *The Long Twentieth Century: Money, Power and the Origins of Our Times*, London and New York 2010. The size of a country's financial markets is one of the most important determinants of safe-haven status; this is one reason why Arrighi's *translatio imperii* moves from city-states to larger and larger nation states. See also Maurizio Michael Habib et al., 'The Fundamentals of Safe Assets', *Journal of International Money and Finance*, vol. 102, April 2020.

and Japan's sovereign debts—the decline of the 'leading safe issuer' real rates accelerates over time.[15] If we look only at the last 500 years, the rate falls by about 1.5 per cent per century; over the last 200 years, it drops by about 2.1 per cent per century. Projecting the post-Napoleonic trend forward through the 2020s, the forecast is that the US—today's leading safe-asset provider—will be permanently stuck with short-term real rates at or below zero by the end of this decade. Fluctuations at business-cycle frequencies—in particular those associated with inflation—may show up as blips when the safe-rate comes up for air; but zero or below is the central tendency of the long-tern trend. 'Global' long-term real rates will follow by the second half of the century.

In other words, the increasing frequency and geographic extent of ZIRPS in the last few decades are not simply the results of the financial crisis and the pandemic. Involving the interaction of multiple factors, they have been a long time in the making. In order to understand these causes, we need to track interest rates on several time horizons at once. We will skip over many exciting episodes in the history of public debt, since in this article we are only interested in causes whose duration persists to the present day. We start out with the largest canvas possible, the whole history of sovereign debt, and proceed from there to periods with shorter and shorter durations as we approach the future, each period ending with the present. This gives the story a telescopic quality, with each period nested deeper in the narrative structure than the last. Proceeding this way will help us understand the acceleration of the 'leading safe issuer' rate over time, as well as explaining some anomalies in the mid-20th century. As cause layers on top of cause, we will see that the tendency to decline is likely to remain with us into the foreseeable future. But we begin at the beginning, with the birth of sovereign debt.

3. EUROPEAN CRUCIBLES

Because sovereign debt is extremely rare in world history, it is easy to pinpoint its emergence. Indeed, it is a sufficiently important watershed that scholars have defined the dividing line between premodern and modern

---

[15] It is important to note here that the results are robust to the way this average is constructed. The theoretically correct approach weights each country by its GDP (the results reported above), but since historical reconstructions of national accounts are sometimes of dubious quality, it is also necessary to check if weighting by population and weighting each country equally return similar results. They do.

fiscal regimes as signalled by 'the widespread appearance of sovereign borrowing'.[16] Public debt only came on the scene in the second half of the 13th century, and only in small pockets of Europe. Understanding why, and what caused it to spread from there, will give us our first clues to understanding the tendency of the rate of interest to fall.

Following Schumpeter, the scholarship known as the New Fiscal Sociology explains the emergence of public debt by way of state capacity.[17] Whereas the 'domain-states' of feudal Europe were too feeble to do more than extract grain from peasants, the 'tax-states' that emerged during the Renaissance could impose monetary standards on their subjects and extract enough from them that debt repayment became plausible, encouraging merchants both to lend and to trade the debt on secondary markets. Between economic growth and political scaling-up, this literature suggests, the emergence of public debt was an inevitable, or at least natural, development.

But while state capacity is no doubt part of the story, it cannot be the whole explanation for the birth of sovereign borrowing. The constraints on fiscal extraction in feudal domains were not binding in other times and places in the ancient and non-European worlds, yet no other states developed long-term public debt at anything like the European scale. As late as the 1780s, China had no public debt—not because it was too weak, but precisely because it was so strong. The Qing empire could simply move resources across space—from a province where there was no war or famine to one where there was—by taxing local elites as needed; it saw no reason to resort to the complicated financial mechanisms that European states employed to move resources through

---

[16] Andrew Monson and Walter Scheidel, eds, *Fiscal Regimes and the Political Economy of Premodern States*, Cambridge 2015, p. 4.

[17] Jürgen Backhaus, ed., *Essays on Fiscal Sociology*, Bern 2005; Richard Bonney, ed., *Economic Systems and State Finance*, Oxford 1995, and *The Rise of the Fiscal State in Europe, c. 1200–1815*, Oxford 1999; Stephan Epstein, *Freedom and Growth: The Rise of States and Markets in Europe, 1300–1750*, London 2000; Isaac William Martin, Ajay Mehrotra and Monica Prasad, eds, *The New Fiscal Sociology: Taxation in Comparative and Historical Perspective*, Cambridge 2009; Kathryn Norberg and Philip Hoffman, eds, *Fiscal Crises, Liberty and Representative Government, 1450–1789*, Stanford 2002; Mark Ormrod, Margaret Bonney, Richard Bonney, eds, *Crises, Revolutions and Self-Sustained Growth: Essays in European Fiscal History, 1130–1830*, Stanford 1999; Bartolomé Yun-Casalilla, Francisco Comín Comín, Patrick K. O'Brien, *The Rise of Fiscal States: A Global History, 1500–1914*, Cambridge 2012.

time.[18] So we can start by asking, why did European states pioneer long-term sovereign borrowing?

The American political scientist David Stasavage identifies four conditions for the emergence of public debt: first, a monetary source of state revenue, ensuring it could repay its debts (many ancient and non-European empires simply employed *corvée* or took delivery of taxes in kind, as did feudal lords); second, large shocks to immediate spending requirements, which required revenue smoothing (in Europe, these shocks were wars); third, the decline of feudal service and citizen militias in favour of professional mercenaries and standing armies, so that meeting the challenge of war led to spending, rather than conscription; and finally, the expectation that rulers would be both willing and able to honour their debts, so that merchant property wasn't simply being confiscated.[19] Stasavage's second condition, spending shocks, turns out to be the key to understanding where safe assets came from and how they evolved.

Despite a far-reaching debate over what (if anything) made Europe's political economy unique, the one contrast that revisionist scholarship has not been able to dislodge is the relative political fragmentation and violence of the European state system.[20] After the fall of Rome, no state

---

[18] Philip Hoffman, *Why Did Europe Conquer the World?*, Princeton 2015, p. 152; Kenneth Pomeranz, *The Great Divergence: China, Europe and the Making of the Modern World Economy*, Princeton 2000, p. 196.

[19] David Stasavage, 'Why Did Public Debt Originate in Europe?', in Andrew Monson and Walter Scheidel, eds, *Fiscal Regimes and the Political Economy of Premodern States*, Cambridge 2015, pp. 523–35.

[20] In *The Great Divergence*, Kenneth Pomeranz set out to dismantle all prior claims about preexisting differences between Europe and China thought to explain their 19th-century economic divergence, yet the unique violence of the European state system was integral even to Pomeranz's arguments: see chapter 4. See also Prasannan Parthasarathi, *Why Europe Grew Rich and Asia Did Not: Global Economic Divergence, 1600–1850*, Cambridge 2011, for the Indian comparison. After Braudel's *Capitalism and Civilization, 15th–18th Century*, vol. 2, chapter 5, the most systematic case for the importance of political plurality is Walter Scheidel, *Escape from Rome: The Failure of Empire and the Road to Prosperity*, Princeton 2019. The objection registered by Steve Pincus and James Robinson—namely, that British fiscal evolution was as much the result of developmentalist strategies as it was due to the needs of war-making—need not contradict this: Pincus and Robinson, 'Wars and State-Making Reconsidered: The Rise of the Developmental State', *Annales*, vol. 71, no. 1, 2017, pp. 9–34.

ever claimed more than 20 per cent of the European population, and most claimed far less.[21] Hundreds of states, most no more than cities with a humble rural periphery, filled the vacuum. These states were engaged in constant, intense warfare against equally powerful opponents from the high Middle Ages on; their numbers over time winnowed only by attrition. Comparing the percentage of years during which states were at war between 1500 and 1800, France (52 per cent), England/Great Britain (53 per cent), Spain (81 per cent) appear roughly comparable to China (56 per cent); but when wars against nomads are excluded the Chinese figures drop to a mere 3 per cent, lower even than the comparatively pacific Austrian dominions (24 per cent).[22]

As a result of constant, intense fighting, the European military apparatus improved substantially, both in terms of hardware and technique. And the most important military technology, by far, was finance. How else are we to account for the survival of a city-state like Venice, deep into the early-modern period, despite the production and population advantages of their neighbours? Tax revenues were roughly equal between major combatants such as France and Spain in the 16th century, or France and Britain in the 18th; and the smaller states like the British and Dutch could borrow more, which compensated for their size. War ate up as much as 7 per cent of GDP in France and 12 per cent in Britain in the 1780s, well over twice, and by some measures three times, the figures for China. As a result, Britain and France in the 1780s each took in more total revenue than China, despite having populations less than one tenth the size, with the vast majority of it going to military engagements. In 1776, per capita taxation measured in grams of silver differed by orders of magnitude between China (7g), France (61g) and Britain (180g). The competitive state system that emerged in Europe in the early-modern period selected for fiscal-military states which were capable of paying for

---

[21] 'The proportion of Europeans ruled by Rome, some 80 percent or more, was similar to the share of population claimed by the largest empires of several other macro-regions, such as those of the Achaemenids and Umayyads (~80 percent) and the Ottomans (~60 percent) in the Middle East and North Africa region; the Maurya, Delhi, and Mughal empires (~90 percent) and the Gupta and Harsha empires (~60 percent) in South Asia; and various Chinese dynasties in East Asia (~80–90 percent).' Scheidel, *Escape from Rome*, p. 219.
[22] Hoffman, *Why Did Europe Conquer the World?*, p. 70.

the shocks of war. 'Safe assets' came into the world dripping from head to toe, from every pore, with blood and dirt.[23]

A second clue regarding the origins of long-term public debt is that the northern Italian city states led the way in issuing these securities. Territorial monarchs sometimes took out direct loans from merchants, but they were usually very short-maturity instruments, no more than one or two years, with double-digit interest rates to compensate for the high risks involved. Henry III's 1345 default on the Tuscan bankers during the Hundred Years' Wars is the traditional example of how easily kings could ruin great banking families like the Bardi and Peruzzi in this period.[24] As a result, little debt was sustainable at scale. Instead, it was republican city-states like Florence, Genoa and Venice that invented large, long-term public debt that could be traded on secondary markets.[25] These polities had several features that made them uniquely well-suited to meeting Stasavage's fourth condition: reputation, combined with administrative capacity for repayment. The political elites staffing their representative assemblies overlapped heavily with the merchants who funded state debt. Small territories limited the influence of landlords, who were usually not creditors themselves, and who in larger territorial assemblies like France's Estates General were capable of taking independent positions on debt repayment and hence of advocating for default when it suited them—which ruined reputations.

Moreover, the compact geography of the city states meant that monitoring costs were low: representatives could meet frequently to supervise state finances, while merchants could intervene directly in the details of tax collection and state expenditure, disciplining anything that threatened repayment. In the larger territories, transportation and communication costs were high; after the collapse of the Roman Empire,

---

[23] Hoffman, *Why Did Europe Conquer the World?*, pp. 49, 20, 70, 51. See also Charles Tilly, *Coercion, Capital and European States, AD 990–1990*, Hoboken 1992; Geoffrey Parker, *The Military Revolution: Military Innovation and the Rise of the West, 1500–1800*, Cambridge 1996.

[24] John Munro, 'The Medieval Origins of the "Financial Revolution": Usury, Rentes and Negotiability', *International History Review*, vol. 25, no. 3, 2003, pp. 505–62. Technically these loans were usually issued as annuities to get around the Catholic ban on usury.

[25] Frederic Lane, *Venice, A Maritime Republic*, Baltimore 1973.

the European road system decayed continuously right down to the 12th century, and major improvements only arrived late in the 18th century. There was no bridge across the Rhine at Cologne, for instance, until the coming of the railroad in the 19th century.[26] This made bourgeois monitoring and intervention much less effective and lending much riskier and more expensive—so much so as to be untenable.

Experiments in public debt propagated outwards from these commercial centres in Northern Italy. In the 13th century, cities in the Low Countries and northern France began borrowing heavily; towns in Germany, Switzerland and Catalonia followed suit in the 14th century. Eventually, the absolute monarchies learned how to use their cities to their advantage.[27] In the late 15th century, Castile under Charles V began issuing public debt through a syndicate of eighteen towns in the Netherlands which had independent control of revenue collection and debt repayments. In 1522 the French crown began experiments along similar lines, using Paris. Castile under Phillip II was the first kingdom to achieve a large domestic public debt, which by some estimates grew to 50 per cent of GDP.[28] From the 1580s, the Dutch Republic could institute its own version of the Italian system, in part because the united provinces were small and run by merchants; in part because the Spanish had been running their municipal-cum-absolutist financial system through Dutch cities for centuries, but also because the united provinces were small, merchant-run and, thanks to their waterways and compact geography, easily accessible: the Hague was no more than a day's travel from the other major cities. The discourse of Anglo-Scottish political economy arose in part as a response to the Dutch challenge, ultimately triumphing in institutional form—after half a century of revolution, counter-revolution and civil war—with the founding of the Bank of England, as a rival to the Bank of Amsterdam, and the establishment of Whig political power to protect it.[29]

---

[26] David Stasavage, *States of Credit: Size, Power and the Development of European Polities*, Princeton 2011, p. 51.

[27] John Hicks, *A Theory of Economic History*, Oxford 1973, chapter 6.

[28] Carlos Álvarez-Nogal and Christophe Chamley, 'Debt Policy Under Constraints: Philip II, the Cortes and Genoese Bankers', *Economic History Review*, vol. 67, no. 1, 2014, pp. 192–213.

[29] John Brewer, *Sinews of Power: War, Money and the English State, 1688–1783*, Cambridge MA 1989; David Stasavage, *Public Debt and the Birth of the Democratic State: France and Great Britain, 1688–1789*, Cambridge 2003. A large literature on

Europe's advantage in the field of public debt was not simply due to its incessantly warring polities generating state demand for finance; the international system was also a source of supply for that credit. Sufficiently reputable sovereign bonds circulated very widely, and that was key to lowering their rates. The city-states couldn't keep up; as late as 1641, only a seventh of Venice's consolidated debt was owned by foreigners, much of the rest being forced loans on citizens; by comparison, the Dutch alone held a full quarter of British debt in 1762.[30] Anyone can issue debts; the challenge is convincing others to accept them. The importance of the international system can be seen by comparing the 'global' average real rate with the 'leading issuer' safe rate, which is always lower. Behind this lies the uneven and combined development of capitalism: second- and third-tier capitalist countries invest in the securities of the leading state, and the demand for safe assets flooding into the leading capitalist state's debt markets grows disproportionately compared to their issuance as the capitalist world-system expands. Thus purely national histories of money do not fully illuminate the history of sovereign debt. Money is indeed socially and politically mediated by

---

'credible commitment' through institutions like liberal property rights and independent central banks has taken off since the classic article by Douglass North and Barry Weingast, 'Constitutions and Commitment: The Evolution of Institutions Governing Public Choice in 17th-Century England', *Journal of Economic History*, vol. 49, no. 4, December 1989, pp. 803–82. However, the statistical tests cited above in Rogoff, Rossi and Schmelzing's 'Long-Run Trends' do not show any trend break associated with the 1688 Glorious Revolution or the 1694 founding of the Bank of England, as the post-Northian literature would expect. This is rather devastating, since the scale of the BoE dataset makes statistical testing for trend breaks especially powerful. Was the theory just wrong? Not necessarily; historians have long been at work to show that the 'financial revolution' associated with the founding of the BoE, originally proclaimed by P. G. M. Dickson, *The Financial Revolution in England: A Study in the Development of Public Credit, 1688–1756*, Berkeley and Los Angeles 1967, was a long, drawn-out process extending over decades, if not centuries. On this longer processual view, see especially Carl Wennerlind, *Casualties of Credit: The English Financial Revolution, 1620–1720*, Cambridge MA 2011 and Christine Desan, *Making Money: Coin, Currency and the Coming of Capitalism*, Oxford 2015, who tracks changes in British common law beginning in the early 17th century.

[30] Luciano Pezzolo, 'The Venetian Government Debt, 1350–1650', in Marc Boone, Karel Davids, Paul Janssens, eds, *Urban Public Debts, Urban Governments and the Market for Annuities in Western Europe, 14th–18th Centuries*, Turnhout 2003, p. 61–74; Arrighi, *Long Twentieth Century*, p. 212. Indeed, by some estimates a full third of all British investment in the 18th century was funded by the Dutch: Matthew Klein and Michael Pettis, *Trade Wars Are Class Wars*, New Haven CT 2020, p. 69.

the state; but the interstate system is determinative for would-be world-monies, and hence for the decline in safe rates we are exploring here.[31]

The combined result of state-and-reputation-building was a fall in the risk premium that creditors charged states over time. This can be demonstrated in three ways. First, as Schmelzing has shown, the weighted average of global real rates converged towards the 'leading safe issuer' real rate at a pace of 0.88 per cent per century, indicating that shrinking risk premia explain much but not all of the overall fall in global real rates in the early-modern period. Second, we can compare sovereign borrowing to other assets considered to offer safe returns at the time, in particular land rents. The 'leading safe issuer' real rate—that of the safest sovereign bond—converged towards land rents at a somewhat slower pace of 0.52 per cent per century. Finally, we can compare interest rates for city-states to those of territorial monarchies. Stasavage estimates that city-states enjoyed a 2 per cent advantage over the monarchies on average in the era of early modernity. Since we know from the first two metrics that risk premia on territorial rates were declining, that 2-point estimate implies a much higher premium in the 15th and 16th centuries and a much lower one by the end of the period, around the mid-18th century.[32]

Thus we can probably say that by the time of Henry Thornton's *Paper Credit* (1802) the leading capitalist state, the British empire, had eliminated most of its default risk premia. Low servicing costs were what allowed Britain to maintain debt levels of over 200 per cent of GDP

---

[31] It is here we must meet neo-chartalist critics. Why did the state, as a central stakeholder, not simply issue tokens in exchange for goods and services and then demand them back in the form of taxes to give the tokens a positive value? Why was it necessary to obtain bullion and other forms of foreign exchange? Although it would take a book to flesh out the case in detail, the answer in short is class conflict within the world-system. Foreign mercenaries did not necessarily pay taxes to the state that employed them, and in any case planned to return home one day; mere tokens, essentially tax credits, would not be enough compensation to risk their lives in battle. A similar argument can be mounted regarding cosmopolitan merchants. Moreover, domestic nobles were not usually comfortable giving the king a monopoly on credit. The classic statement of the chartalist case was Georg Friedrich Knapp's *The State Theory of Money*, London 1924 [Leipzig 1905].

[32] For convergence rates per century, see Schmelzing, 'Eight Centuries of Global Real Interest Rates', p. 28; for city-states' premiums, see David Stasavage, *States of Credit*, p. 17.

during the Napoleonic Wars.[33] And by the time of Bagehot's *Lombard Street* (1873), the City of London's money markets had become quite liquid. It took the long 19th century for the rest of the capitalist core to catch up with the British empire on these metrics. Most central banks were founded much later than England's; indeed the US did not have a permanent central bank until 1913. Even then, taking on their role as lenders of last resort took time and spread unevenly. Before 1914, central banks' principal contributions to lower interest rates happened in times of war, which was not infrequent; it was only after 1945 that responding to peacetime financial panics became the dominant driver of central banks' balance sheets. Making sure that financial assets maintained their value through crises became ever more important as the financial system expanded beyond the regulated confines of mid-century banking to a global system of market-based finance.[34] As waves of liquidity washed over global financial markets, satisfying the preference for liquidity, capitalists began to take advantage of even more modern forms of illiquid investment, complicating the story of interest rates' decline.

4. MODERN CAPITALIST CYCLES

Telescoping now as we consider structures with shorter durations that are bearing down on interest rates today, what accounts for the downward trend and its various accelerations after the crucible of early modernity set the trend towards solid tax states and liquid money markets? This is where the nested periodizations come in handy; for although the early modern period forms a relatively uniform time for rate declines, the modern period, with the onset of industrialized and increasingly urbanized capitalism, is much stranger.

To get a sense of this, let's set real interest rates aside for a moment and return to nominal rates, where some of the statistical features are

---

[33] Patrick O'Brien and Philip Hunt, 'England, 1485–1815', in Bonney, ed., *The Rise of the Fiscal State in Europe*, p. 61. By contrast, the failure of the French state to sustain credible repayment policies due to the Crown's inability to raise taxes is what led to high debt-servicing costs—and ultimately to the default which detonated the Revolution. Gail Bossenga, 'Financial Origins of the French Revolution', in Dale Van Kley and Thomas Kaiser, eds, *From Deficit to Deluge: The Origins of the French Revolution*, Stanford 2011.
[34] Leon Wansleben, *The Rise of Central Banks: State Power in Financial Capitalism*, Cambridge MA 2023.

more visually pronounced, thanks to offsetting effects from deflation (Figure 3, below). Unlike the global real rates, which display a single secular trend for 700 years (*sans* the Black Death and the 1557 rupture), the fall of nominal rates decelerated in the long 19th century. On top of that flatter baseline, we can see two major and two minor cycles of rising rates. The first major cycle is associated with the French Revolution and the Napoleonic Wars; the minor cycles, in the 1860s–70s and the 1910s, are linked respectively to the wars of national unification—American, German, Italian, Japanese—and the First World War. Important as they are for our understanding of world-economic history, these episodes do not have a direct bearing on our situation today. Instead, what calls out for explanation is the major postwar cycle, which is also quite visible in the real rate series and still a problem for us.

As it turns out, these patterns—deceleration of rate declines in the 19th century; a powerful cycle of rising rates in the third quarter of the 20th century—must themselves be further decomposed into multiple over-lapping processes. They are both products of profound but temporary transition periods in the history of capitalism, which have now come to an end. Hence the statistical continuity in the real rate series: from the per-spective of the long history of capitalism, the mid-20th century 'golden age' was merely a blip, which is now reverting to long-term trends.

FIGURE 3: *Global Average of Nominal Interest Rates on Sovereign Debt*

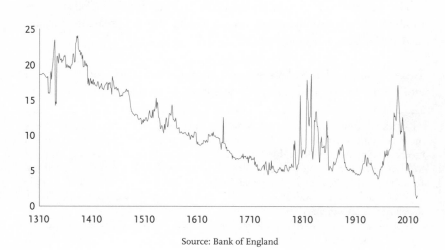

Source: Bank of England

In order to understand these patterns, we need to examine the uneven growth of liquidity, saving and investment over time. To maintain a stable level of aggregate demand, when the desire to save increases, the price of borrowing must decline, while increases in desired investment have the opposite effect—a rise in interest rates. But the propensity to save is universal, constant and strong; under the uncertainty imposed by capitalism, there is no choice but to build up a precautionary buffer stock for bad times.[35] The propensity to invest, on the other hand, is notoriously concentrated, fickle and often rather weak. Why deal with the hassle of productive investment—building a factory, sourcing raw materials, finding buyers, dealing with labour unrest—when it is safe, easy and decently profitable simply to lend to the government by buying bonds? Individuals under capitalism prefer safe, liquid stores of value. The question then becomes: what provokes investment?

5. STAGNATION AND ITS THEORISTS

The long-term stagnation of commercial society has been the subject of debate since the Enlightenment. Smith envisioned a 'stationary state', once the gains from specialization and trade had been exhausted. In a country which 'had acquired that full complement of riches which the nature of its soil and climate, and its situation with respect to other countries, allowed it to acquire; which could, therefore, advance no further, and which was not going backwards, both the wages of labour and the profits of stock [including debt] would probably be very low.' Malthus and Ricardo balanced population growth against land, which was ultimately limited. The Hegelian system refused this classical vision of eventual rest and insisted, with Hobbes, that modernity was characterized by a 'perpetual and restless desire of power after power, that ceaseth only in death'. States could channel this drive into imperialism, aiming to bolster social stability at home; but such a solution would be impossible at a world level.[36]

---

[35] Carroll, 'Buffer-Stock Saving and the Life Cycle/Permanent Income Hypothesis'; Christopher Carroll, Robert Hall and Stephen Zeldes, 'The Buffer-Stock Theory of Saving: Some Macroeconomic Evidence', *Brookings Papers on Economic Activity*, vol. 1992, no. 2, 1992, pp. 61–156; Christopher Carroll and Olivier Jeanne, 'A Tractable Model of Precautionary Reserves, Net Foreign Assets, or Sovereign Wealth Funds', NBER Working Paper No. 15228, 2009.
[36] Albert Hirschman, 'On Hegel, Imperialism and Structural Stagnation', *Journal of Development Economics*, vol. 3, no. 1, March 1976, pp. 1–8.

In 1898, corporate banker and dollar diplomat Charles Conant recycled this view for a mainstream American audience. His magazine article, 'The Economic Basis of "Imperialism"', explained that 'capital congestion' in the core countries pushed interest rates down, 'the result of a natural law of economic and race development' which obliged the more advanced parts of the world to invest in areas that still lacked capital. Nor was the economic crisis of the 1890s, which Conant diagnosed as the result of excess savings with no investment outlet, particularly novel as a world event:

> The Florentine cities found capital accumulating on their hands beyond the capacity for its safe employment and were compelled to make precarious loans to foreign kings. Holland faced a congestion of capital in the days of her great maritime supremacy, when money sought investment in vain at two per cent, and the wild folly of the tulip mania illustrated the tendency to speculation which such conditions foster. England was afflicted with such a congestion of capital in the early days of the Stuarts, when prosperity and commercial greatness began to afford small commercial savings to Englishmen, and again in the middle of the last century, when three per cents were quoted at 107. In each of these cases the world was far from rich, and savings could not be said to exist in excess in the sense that there was more than enough for all. But the question of congested capital is a practical one and not a sentimental one.[37]

If socialism might have relieved capitalism of its congestion, Conant dismissed that option out of hand. War and empire had always been the formula for fiscal expansion, and he saluted the 1898 Spanish-American War as a sign of capitalist maturity and health. During the Great Depression, thinkers across the political spectrum, from Keynes to Schumpeter, took up the problem of capitalist stagnation without such prejudice. The Polish economist Henryk Grossman's *The Law of Accumulation and Breakdown of the Capitalist System* (1929), the jewel in the Frankfurt School's crown before Horkheimer became research director, is a reconsideration of the role of capitalist breakdown theory in the mature Marx. The America Keynesian Alvin Hansen elaborated a widely popular theory of 'secular stagnation', arguing that the closing of the frontier, the demographic transition and the exhaustion of new technologies meant that private investment would no longer be high enough

---

[37] Charles Conant, 'The Economic Basis of "Imperialism"', *North American Review*, vol. 167, no. 502, September 1898, pp. 326–40. On Conant, see also my 'Imperial Fed', *Phenomenal World*, 30 March 2023.

to sustain full employment—hence the need for state investment to pick up the slack.[38]

Hansen's students—including a young Paul Sweezy—elevated his secular stagnation concept into a theory of history. In *An Economic Programme for American Democracy*, seven students from Harvard and Tufts made the case that a new stage in human evolution had arrived, and only full-blown social democracy was up to the task of socializing investment on the scale needed to provide full employment, social stability and modern freedom. The alternative, as far as they could tell, was military government across the Atlantic world and an eventual 'holocaust of slaughter and bloodshed'.[39]

A few years later, exiled in war-time Oxford, the Polish political economist Michał Kalecki laid out his theory of what had gone wrong. Capitalists resisted public investment despite the increased profits that came with it, he explained, because it removed their leverage over society and the state. The social function of 'sound finance' was to make the level of employment depend on the 'state of confidence', he wrote. Under a regime of permanent full employment, 'the sack' would cease to play its role as a disciplinary measure; 'discipline in the factories' and 'political stability' were more important to business leaders than profits.[40] In capitalist societies, therefore, demand management over the course of the business cycle tended instead to take the form of 'stimulating'—or bribing—private investment with cuts in taxes and interest rates. But unless rates were raised during every boom, to provide firepower for the next bust, every new downturn would exert a ratchet effect, causing a jagged downward trend in rates over time—exactly what we see in the data above. Only fascist states—which ensure order in the factories and in the streets—would be capable of raising public investment as a way of ensuring full employment, Kalecki speculated, and only by provoking an arms race, a process which 'ends inevitably in war'.

---

[38] Alvin Hansen, 'Economic Progress and Declining Population Growth,' *American Economic Review*, vol. 29, no. 1, March 1939, pp. 1–15; see also Roger Backhouse and Mauro Boianovsky, 'Secular stagnation: The History of a Macroeconomic Heresy', *European Journal of the History of Economic Thought*, vol. 23, no. 6, 2016.

[39] Richard Gilbert, George Hildebrand Jr., Arthur Stuart, Maxine Yaple Sweezy, Paul Sweezy, Lorie Tarshis and John Wilson, *An Economic Programme for American Democracy*, New York 1938, p. 91.

[40] Michał Kalecki, 'Political Aspects of Full Employment' [1943], in *The Last Phase in the Transformation of Capitalism*, New York 1972.

Prescient as they were, the ideas of Hansen, Kalecki and their followers were quickly set aside after 1945. The *trente glorieuses* and the welfare state appeared to discredit their pessimism, Korea and Vietnam war booms notwithstanding.[41] Today, their thoughts on investment and interest rates seem ahead of their time. Picking up where these thinkers left off, the task now is to understand how, and with what implications, the 21st-century economic system has come to drown in its own liquidity.

6. FAILING INDUCEMENTS

As our telescoping analysis approaches the present, special attention will need to be paid to the US, as the leading and dominant safe-asset provider. As we will see, for the most part what has kept interest rates stable or even rising over the last 150 years has been the result of a series of one-off transitions, which have now come to an end. The period 1945–80 was a very strange sweet spot of overlapping caesuras in the US: the baby boom, income compression and the tail end of the second industrial revolution converged with the power of an organized working class and a sharp, wartime-induced jump in the size of the fiscal state to produce an inflationary expansion. The result was rising nominal (headline) interest rates—but a continued decline in real rates, corrected for inflation. Since most of the conventional wisdom regarding what is 'normal' in capitalist dynamics was formed in the middle of these parentheses, much of it will need to be rethought. As a first step, we can look at trends in what have historically been the four most important inducements to investment, and so to keeping interest rates up: the capitalist frontier, new technology, demographic expansion and consumer demand; these factors become especially important in combination.

The frontier. The frontier has been a constant of capitalist world history, from Siberia to the Amazon.[42] It has always involved an ugly, bloody process of imperial conquest. In the US, the expansion of capitalist space into new territory allowed for the replication of European social formations

---

[41] Tim Barker, 'Macroeconomic Consequences of Peace: American Radical Economists and the Problem of Military Keynesianism, 1938–1975', *Research in the History of Economic Thought and Methodology*, vol. 37, May 2019.

[42] Sven Beckert, Ulbe Bosma, Mindi Schneider and Eric Vanhaute, 'Commodity Frontiers and the Transformation of the Global Countryside: a Research Agenda', *Journal of Global History*, vol. 16, no. 3, pp. 435–50, June 2021.

further west: building more farms, more roads, more city halls. In short, it was an immense provocation to productive investment. When the process of imperial expansion came together with the industrial revolution in the 19th century, the 'settler revolution' went into overdrive. The larger capitalist space made room for a more advanced division of labour; developing commodity chains and a larger market for goods encouraged capitalists to take advantage of increasing returns to scale to sink even more savings into productive investment.[43] As global imperial frontiers closed around 1900, however, and this target for investment receded, rates began to tumble once again; recall Conant's worries about the investment dearth in 1898, which he compared to earlier crises of accumulation in Florence, Holland and England.

Technology. A second factor, however, was waiting in the wings: new technology can induce productive investment. Firms that want to stay competitive, entrepreneurs who fantasize about creating new worlds, and governments that want to keep up with or overtake their rivals may all want to borrow to invest in productive capital.[44] Beginning around 1870, the second industrial revolution induced a massive round of fixed investment that lasted until 1970, after which the gains from exploiting

FIGURE 4: *American Total-Factor Productivity Growth, 1900–2014*

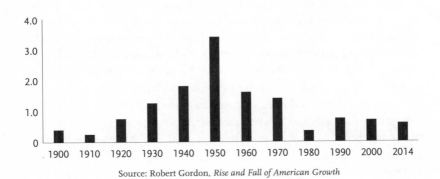

Source: Robert Gordon, *Rise and Fall of American Growth*

[43] James Belich, *Replenishing the Earth: The Settler Revolution and the Rise of the Angloworld, 1783–1939*, Oxford 2009; Jonathan Scott, *How the Old World Ended: The Anglo–Dutch–American Revolution, 1500–1800*, New Haven CT 2020; Steven Topik and Allen Wells, *Global Markets Transformed, 1870–1945*, Cambridge MA 2014.
[44] Antonin Bergeaud, Gilbert Cette and Rémy Lecat, 'The Circular Relationship Between Productivity Growth and Real Interest Rates', Banque de France Working Paper, no. 734, October 2019.

the new technology began to hit diminishing returns (Figure 4). Since then, the advanced economies have seen falling investment rates. Firms have been less eager to update or expand their capital equipment. The upward pressure on rates exerted by investment in industrial technology has slackened.[45]

The slowdown in productivity growth corresponds to the industrial transition of western economies into the service sector, which has had multiple compounding effects on investment. The transition has changed the nature of capital itself, slowing private-sector dynamics and altering the mechanics of aggregate demand management by the state. Since service work is often not amenable to technological upgrading, it requires less rapid turnover of capital equipment and hence less overall investment. This means that central banks no longer need to struggle to hold back inflationary investment booms with rate hikes, relieving upward pressure on interest rates.[46] Further relaxing inflationary investment pressures, the prices of capital goods have been falling relentlessly from at least the 1950s onward, allowing any given amount of investment spending to go further, reducing the total outlays required to keep pace with changing market conditions. By one measure, the price of capital goods has fallen by as much as 75 per cent in the last seventy years.[47]

In addition, monetary policy has become less effective as a tool for fighting downturns in the service economy. Every downturn requires a stronger response than the last, in order to compensate for declining monetary-policy efficacy, exerting a downward ratchet effect on interest rates. In part, this is because the composition of investment spending has shifted: investment categories that are interest-rate sensitive—equipment, durables, structures—are less salient today, while categories that are not interest-rate sensitive, intellectual property in particular, have become more important. In the US, IP investments were

---

[45] Robert Gordon, *The Rise and Fall of American Growth: The US Standard of Living since the Civil War*, Princeton 2017.
[46] Aaron Benanav, *Automation and the Future of Work*, London and New York 2020; Dietrich Vollrath, *Fully Grown: Why a Stagnant Economy Is a Sign of Success*, Chicago 2020.
[47] William Collins and Jeffrey Williamson, 'Capital Goods Prices and Investment, 1879–1950', *Journal of Economic History*, vol. 61, no. 1, 2001, pp. 59–94; Robert Gordon, *The Measurement of Durable Goods Prices*, Chicago 1990. For the 75 per cent estimate of the fall in capital goods' prices: Barry Eichengreen, 'Secular Stagnation: The Long View', *American Economic Review*, vol. 105, no. 5, May 2015, p. 68.

less than 1 per cent of GDP in the 1950s; today they constitute at least 5 per cent. Since IP investments are less sensitive to interest rates—pharmaceutical companies, for example, keep their scientists working all year round, regardless of market conditions—monetary authorities must step harder on the gas, lowering rates further to achieve the same level of recovery.[48]

Finally, capital goods are now produced globally and many are imported—a state of affairs more reminiscent of the pre-1914 world than of the mid-century's self-contained national economies. One upshot is that investment spending no longer boosts domestic employment, wages or consumption as strongly as in the past. Imported capital goods accounted for only 3.5 per cent of equipment investment in 1967, but by 2008 had risen tenfold to 36 per cent; for 'equipment and durables', the import share has increased from 7 to 42 per cent since 1960. Whereas an extra $100 of investment spending generated $60 worth of domestic wages in 1966, this had fallen to $45 by 2010.[49] Again, this means that central bank interest-rate policy has lost much of its kick—as much as 38 per cent from these two sources alone—as a tool for fighting recessions, contributing to the downwards ratchet effect which we observe in the data. Not only is it harder for monetary policy to create investment in our globalized service economy, but what investment spending it can induce does not generate as much in employment, wages or consumption.

Demographic expansion. The third factor that has historically encouraged investment is population growth. This is similar in certain ways to the capitalist frontier. Instead of a community expanding across space as

---

[48] Justin Bloesch and Jacob Weber, 'Structural Changes in Investment and the Waning Power of Monetary Policy', Harvard Economics Working Paper, 22 March 2021. See also Herman Mark Schwartz, 'Global Secular Stagnation and the Rise of Intellectual Property Monopoly', *Review of International Political Economy*, vol. 29, no. 5, 2022, pp. 1448–76 on the social and institutional foundations of corporate IP strategy.

[49] The calculation of domestic wages/investment is as follows. An extra $1 of investment spending on capital good A will directly produce domestic labour income equal to: (labour share of income in the capital good A sector)*(1 - import share of all spending on capital good A). Accounting for the slight fall in the labour share in the equipment and durables sectors, we have the following for our two time periods: $0.6 (=.65*.93) and $0.35 (=.6*.58). The higher figure of $45 given in the main text is accounted for by the rise of IP, which has both a higher labour share and a smaller import share. The complete calculation is given by Bloesch and Weber, 'Structural Changes', which includes allowances for depreciation and consumption-multiplier effects.

borders are pushed out, a population growing through time can induce investment as capitalists bump up against capacity constraints, money income grows more rapidly and firms expand to exploit the larger consumer base. Both accelerated consumption growth and rising investment rates tend to push interest rates up. The so-called 'settling of the West' in America was both an expansion of boundaries and an increase in population, pushed along by massive waves of immigration. The restrictions on immigration that America put into effect in 1924, however, compounded the effects of the closing of the global frontiers three decades earlier. The demographic decline that worried Hansen in the 1930s was largely self-imposed.

Globally, the 'demographic transition'—a reduction in death rates, with birth rates falling even further—happened unevenly; there was no correlation with either immigration or frontiers. Its ultimate effect, however, has been slower population growth in the advanced economies. A short baby boom after World War II initially reversed this trend, contributing to the postwar 'Golden Age' of capitalism, as companies expanded capacity to service the larger consumer market. But well before the end of the 20th century, this too had fizzled out. We are thus at the end of the second major caesura in the history of capitalism: the massive demographic expansion after the lifting of the Malthusian constraint is now being followed by a period of reduced fertility. The peak in global population-growth rates, 2 per cent a year, was reached at the end of the 1960s. Since then, the global fertility rate has dropped from 4.5 to 2.5—just over the 2.1 required to maintain a constant population—and consequently population growth had fallen to 1.2 per cent by 2015. In the coming decades, the UN expects a decrease globally, with East Asia entering full-scale demographic decline in the 2030s; South Asian population growth is projected to peak in the 2060s; while sub-Saharan Africa will continue to grow until the end of the 21st century, but with a quickening deceleration starting before 2050.[50]

---

[50] UN, *World Population Prospects 2022*. These projections constitute an upper-bound because the UN demographic modelling on which they are based is almost certainly wildly misspecified. Since the 1950s they have used deterministic trends to model fertility, death and migration patterns; only since 2010 have they introduced stochastic variations that allow for some estimation of uncertainty in forecasts. The paper by Stein Emil Vollset et al., 'Fertility, Mortality, Migration and

In the 21st century, populations are declining all across the advanced world. Japan is in the vanguard, which may have contributed to its pioneering ZIRPs in the 1990s, a decade before the West. Europe is close behind, and China will soon face crushing demographic pressures. The Chinese labour force has been shrinking since 2017, and its total population has now entered decline as well. China's population is forecast to fall by about 6 million annually in the mid-2040s, and by 12 million a year by the late 2050s. Among the great powers, only America is set to grow its population over the course of the full 21st century, largely thanks to immigration, regularly reformed since 1964.[51]

Economists, demographers and government statistical agencies agree that there is not much prospect for this trend reversing. Pro-natalist policies are being implemented in a growing number of countries, but the evidence continues to indicate that they simply do not work; any short-term boosts to birth rates are followed by a long-term return to trend.[52] Economic models of fertility suggest that, as household income rises, families choose to have more children; but also that, as women's income increases—as occurred with the accelerated entry of women into the American labour force, starting in the 1960s—fertility declines; even as cross-sectional patterns have changed in recent decades, the overall timeseries facts remain the same.[53] But the main variables, accounting for over 80 per cent of the variation in fertility across countries, are female education levels and access to birth control. It is no mystery then why the largest drops in fertility have been observed among teenagers, or why most of the drop is the result of decline in first births, rather

Population Scenarios for 195 Countries and Territories from 2017 to 2100', *Lancet*, vol. 396, 1 October 2020, is a more sophisticated source of projections about future demography, predicting sharper slowdowns and larger outright declines. I use the conservative UN numbers, already stark enough, as an upper bound, to avoid cherry-picking projections for catastrophism.
[51] United Nations, Department of Economic and Social Affairs, Population Division (2022). *World Population Prospects 2022: Online Edition;* Pew Research Center, 'Modern Immigration Wave Brings 59 Million to US Driving Population Growth and Change Through 2065: Views of Immigration's Impact on US Society Mixed', Washington DC, September 2015.
[52] Elizabeth Brainerd, 'Can Government Policies Reverse Undesirable Declines in Fertility?', *IZA World of Labour*, May 2014.
[53] Matthias Doepke, Anne Hannusch, Fabian Kindermann and Michèle Tertilt, 'The Economics of Fertility: A New Era', NBER Working Paper, no. 29948, April 2022.

than in second or third births.[54] The demographic transition is a major cultural accomplishment.

What effects will the new demographic regime have on interest rates? Slower population growth means fewer consumers for firms to prepare to sell to by investing in new capacity, but it also means fewer savers to validate that investment ex-post. Considered only in aggregate, the two forces might cancel out their opposite impacts on interest rates. More consequential are the knock-on effects of slowing population growth on the age distribution. In the later phases of the demographic transition, the mass of the population shifts upwards and older segments of the population bulk larger in the economic field. Over-50s have increased their average share of the world population from 15 to 25 per cent since the 1950s; it is expected to be 40 per cent by 2100. There is a composition effect, in terms of how many people are young, middle-aged or retired: fewer young people borrowing money to begin their lives, and more 50-somethings building up their life-time savings prior to retirement, means less desired investment and more desired saving—an unambiguous downward pressure on interest rates.[55]

Might the increase in the number of retired people (who are dissaving) offset that downward pressure? Not as forcefully as some pessimistic imaginations suggest. Since the 1990s there has been a persistent fear of 'asset-market meltdown', as boomers retire and withdraw their savings from the financial system, pushing interest rates up and asset valuations down. The experience of Japan, and the absence of such a downward spiral, convinced many observers that this was off-base. The argument has recently been revived as the 'great demographic reversal', suggesting that Japan may have been an exception, given that its demographic decline could be offset by offshoring parts of its industrial base to growing China—while today, the entire advanced world is looking at demographic stagnation.[56] But this overstates the case. In the US, for

[54] Melissa Kearney, Phillip Levine and Luke Pardue, 'The Puzzle of Falling US Birth Rates since the Great Recession', *Journal of Economic Perspectives*, vol. 36, no. 1, Winter 2022.

[55] Adrien Auclert, Hannes Malmberg, Frederic Martenet and Matthew Rognlie, 'Demographics, Wealth and Global Imbalances in the Twenty-First Century', NBER Working Paper, no. 29161.

[56] Charles Goodhart and Manoj Pradhan, *The Great Demographic Reversal: Ageing Societies, Waning Inequality and an Inflation Revival*, New York 2020.

example, the bell curve for age is gently shifting upwards—the median age was 28 in 1968 and has risen to 38 today; it is projected to be 42 in 2065—not exploding into the 70s as boomers retire.[57] Since 40- and 50-year-olds are on average more productive, make more money, have higher savings accumulated as they approach retirement, and are living longer, the upshot is likely to be higher capital-output ratios for the world as a whole. Finally, while there are obvious intuitive reasons to imagine that retirees are on-net dissavers, empirically this is more suspect: movement in the size of the savings accumulated by retirees is overdetermined by the vast wealth of the top 1 per cent, who tend to pursue a strategy of maintaining their hoards into very old age, the better to endow the next generation of their dynasty.[58]

There is significant debate about the magnitude of demographic trends' weight on interest rates. Estimates range from declines of 1 to 3 per cent—large numbers, given the 20th-century average of 2 per cent real returns on long-term US Treasuries—with the most sophisticated models closer to the middle and lower end of the spectrum.[59] This dispersion reflects real differences of opinion, data and modelling strategy, on the part of researchers; but it is also expressive of the unevenness of the demographic transition itself. Countries' populations are changing at differential rates, with differential implications for the dynamics of capital. This will likely worsen global imbalances, with downward pressures on interest rates greatest at the centre of the capitalist world system. In particular, the rising demand for safe assets from the rest of the world will put pressure on American capital markets, so that US rates will not just feel the effects of the domestic demographic transition; Wall Street and the Treasury will be faced with demand for safe assets from the entire ageing world.

---

[57] Pew Research Center, 'Modern Immigration Wave Brings 59 Million to US, Driving Population Growth and Change Through 2065'.

[58] Atif Mian, Ludwig Straub and Amir Sufi, 'What Explains the Decline in r^*? Rising Income Inequality versus Demographic Shifts', *Proceedings of the 2021 Jackson Hole Symposium*, August 2021.

[59] Etienne Gagnon, Benjamin Johannsen and David López-Salido, 'Understanding the New Normal: The Role of Demographics', *IMF Economic Review*, March 2021, estimate that demographics accounted for a decline of 1 per cent of real interest rates between 1970 and 2015, while Gauti Eggertsson, Neil Mehrotra and Jacob Robbins, 'A Model of Secular Stagnation: Theory and Quantitative Evaluation', *American Economic Journal: Macroeconomics*, vol. 11, no. 1, January 2019, suggest the 3 per cent figure.

Consumer purchasing power. Finally, the income and wealth compression of the mid-century moment created a massive consumer market in the US that induced productive investment to satisfy the new middle classes. Since the onset of the neoliberal period, however, the problem of excess savings has been exacerbated by the rise of inequality. Those at the top of the income scale save much more of their income than workers whose consumption is essentially hand-to-mouth. The macroeconomic consequences for interest rates of this changing balance of class power are only just beginning to be explored econometrically.

Between 1953 and 2019, microdata from the *Survey of Consumer Finances (Plus)* shows that whereas the top 10 per cent save 20 per cent of their income in an average year, the next 40 per cent save barely 8 per cent, while the bottom 50 per cent are able to save a mere 1.5 per cent.[60] As inequality worsens, this produces a 'savings glut of the rich'.[61] But the rich cannot lend if no one wants to borrow. Without additional investment to soak up the new desired savings of the rich—absent for all the reasons discussed above—either growth must slow or someone else must dissave. The role of the neo-rentier—lending to the lower classes, to enable them to continue to consume through indebtedness—has become an increasingly attractive proposition, as banks have produced new financial instruments that have promised to make such lending less risky. To induce that extra borrowing, interest rates must fall. On its own, the 'rise of the 1 per cent' over the last forty years is estimated to account for real rate declines of between 0.45 and 0.85 per cent.[62]

7. RETURN OF HISTORY

Inter-imperial competition; the radical uncertainty which causes a preference for liquidity and leads the propensity to save to overwhelm the propensity to invest; the exhaustion of frontiers; demographic transition; high and rising levels of inequality; business-cycle management—these processes are internal to capitalist development.

[60] Mian, Straub and Sufi, 'What Explains the Decline in r^*?', p. 15. See also Adrien Auclert and Matthew Rognlie, 'Aggregate Demand and the Top 1 Percent', *American Economic Review*, vol. 107, no. 5, May 2017; Auclert and Rognlie, 'Inequality and Aggregate Demand', NBER Working Paper, no. 24280, January 2020.
[61] Atif Mian, Ludwig Straub and Amir Sufi, 'The Saving Glut of the Rich', NBER Working Paper, no. 26941, April 2020.
[62] Auclert and Rognlie, 'Aggregate Demand and the Top 1 Percent'.

Each has its own periodicity, occurring at a distinct speed and rhythm, and its own time horizon. But layer each of these periods on top of one another and it becomes clear that capitalist time has a powerful directionality to it, which displays a distinct feature, namely a tendency for the rate of interest to fall. Today, as nominal rates hit their effective lower bound with increasing frequency and—beneath today's brief uptick of headline rates—the pressures for real rate declines continue unabated, our times appear to be opening up. Although it will likely be with us for a while longer, capitalist directionality presents itself as more of a problem than a guide. What are we to do in a world where liquid capital is becoming abundant?

We can sketch at least three scenarios going forward. First, some new set of general-purpose technologies—efficient batteries? quantum computing? carbon capture? space travel?—might induce productive private investment, temporarily restoring the scarcity-value of capital as it is channelled into new enterprises. A surprise second baby boom or a reform of the PRC's *hukou* system could have a similar effect. Waves of this kind have caused ripples on the stream of capitalist time before, sometimes lasting generations. Ultimately, though, this would only prolong the contradictions, not resolve them.

Without the normal stabilization mechanisms that the capitalist state has come to rely on for managing the 20th-century business cycle, the 21st century may simply have a permanently depressed economy: low investment, low employment, low wages, each compounding the others as demographic decline, technological stagnation and rising inequality push savings and investment schedules farther and farther apart. The implied social chaos and resulting political pressures make this the least likely outcome. Instead, fiscal policy is likely to play a much larger role in capitalist stabilization going forward. This was always an option, but it was largely foreclosed outside the context of war and pandemic, for reasons outlined by Kalecki.[63] However, neoliberal elites rocked by a decade of populist uprisings have begun to change course. What begins as meliorism may not be sufficient to contain the noise and tumult of

---

[63] See Thomas Oatley, *A Political Economy of American Hegemony: Buildups, Booms and Busts*, Cambridge 2015, for a statistical analysis of the exclusively bellicist origins of American fiscal policy. On the role of mass warfare in generating confiscatory taxes on western elites, see Kenneth Scheve and David Stasavage, *Taxing the Rich: A History of Fiscal Fairness in the United States and Europe*, Princeton 2016.

capitalist breakdown as the real rate of interest sinks deeper and deeper into negative territory. Faced with a widening gap between what monetary policy alone can achieve and what citizens expect, even politicians who want to preserve economic hierarchies will look for ways to stabilize the social system with the state. They are likely to decide that everything must change so that everything can stay the same.

Between the Infrastructure, Investment and Jobs Act, CHIPS and the Inflation Reduction Act, the Biden Administration is making forays into this kind of politics, as the Trump Administration had already begun to do. Though nominal rates have been rising in tandem with the current business cycle, this is unlikely to continue. When the temporary inflationary impulses stemming from the pandemic and war in Ukraine recede, interest rates will stabilize until the next cyclical turn. Meanwhile the slow and steady pressures of the *longue durée* will continue to assert themselves. To bridge the growing gap between stability and declining real rates, capitalist states must continue to socialize investment.

Exactly what forms that socialization process will take, however, are up for grabs. The second scenario, as militarist Keynesianism once again rears its ugly head around the world, would be no cause for celebration. Recall the 'slaughter and bloodshed' foreseen by the Tufts and Harvard students in 1938. Politics, not history or economics, will decide what happens on this new terrain of struggle. A third scenario would see the mobilization of alternative ideas for public investments. These might include green energy, public education, public housing, infrastructure, reparations for racial and climate justice, childcare, robust supply chains to unclog potentially inflationary bottlenecks and productivity improvements in the service sector. These are areas in which we all have a collective interest.

Politically, the ruling classes are as strong as ever. Economically, despite—and indeed sometimes because of—their projects to keep capital scarce, they have backed themselves into a corner of capital abundance and are frequently begging to purchase public debt, even at negative rates. What kind of world is it that can stand zero per cent returns on short- and, increasingly, long-term liquid capital for such a long time? The answer would seem to be one in which capital is digging its own grave. As the primary tool for state management increasingly hits its limits in the form of the zero-lower bound, either capitalism will become increasingly unstable, or some other stabilization mechanism will be found. Unless we want a worsening repeat of the 2010s, the world of liquid capital abundance that is coming into being will require more economic planning than ever. This upshot is breathing life back into one of the classical arguments for socialism: historical necessity. The thesis that history has a direction was knocked out of court by the capitalist triumphalism of the 1990s, when the fall of the Soviet Union and attacks from postmodernism cornered many into conceding 'the global contingency of social temporality'.[64] For a few decades, time seemed to be open-ended but not progressive. Since the global financial crisis, the prospect of being stuck in the capitalist present has become increasingly unbearable. It is time to set aside the notion that capital is scarce and begin imagining what that might mean for our future.

---

[64] William Sewell Jr, 'The Capitalist Epoch', *Social Science History*, vol. 38, nos. 1–2, Spring–Summer 2014.

Schelling's Late Philosophy in Confrontation with Hegel

Peter Dews

- Provides a detailed and lucid examination of Schelling's late philosophical system

- Presents a sustained, systematic discussion of the differences between Schelling's late philosophy and the philosophy of Hegel

- Maps Schelling's intellectual development from his early writings, through his middle-period work, to the threshold of the late system

This book is the first in English to survey the whole of Schelling's late system, and to explore in detail the rationale for its division into a "negative philosophy" and a "positive philosophy." It begins by tracing Schelling's intellectual development from his early work of the 1790s up to the threshold of his final phase. It then examines Schelling's mature conception of the scope of pure thinking, the basis of negative philosophy, and the nature of the transition to positive philosophy. In this second, historically oriented enterprise Schelling explores the deep structure of mythological worldviews and seeks to explain the epochal shift to the modern universe of "revelation."

Simultaneously, the book offers a sustained comparison of Hegel's and Schelling's treatment of a range of central topics in post-Kantian thought: the relation between a priori thinking and being; the role of religion in human existence; the inner dynamics of history; and the paradoxical structure of freedom.

About the author

Peter Dews taught philosophy at the University of Essex for several decades before becoming Emeritus Professor in 2018. He has also held visiting positions in the United States, Germany, and Brazil. He has published widely on modern French philosophy, the Frankfurt School, and the major thinkers of German Idealism.

 Follow us @OUPPhilosophy

REVIEWS

Martin Wolf, *The Crisis of Democratic Capitalism*
Allen Lane: London 2023, £30, hardback
496 pp, 978 0 2413 034 12

DYLAN RILEY

SERMONS FOR PRINCES

If democratic capitalism is in crisis, Martin Wolf, chief economics commentator at the *Financial Times*, would seem well placed to plumb the reasons why. Wolf is an extraordinarily well-connected and well-informed writer—'the world's pre-eminent financial journalist', as Lawrence Summers's backhanded compliment would have it. Two features distinguish him from his American counterparts. The first is that his columns are of a far higher intellectual calibre than, say, a Paul Krugman's. The second is that in the US, it would be expected that an economist of Wolf's standing would also occupy a named chair at an Ivy League university and rotate through roles in the Treasury–Federal Reserve nexus. That does not apply in the Westminster system. Though central bankers and financiers feature prominently among the close friends and interlocutors thanked in his books—Mervyn King, Ben Bernanke, Olivier Blanchard, Raghuram Rajan, Andy Haldane, Jeffrey Sachs, George Soros—in *The Crisis of Democratic Capitalism*, Wolf declares himself proud to be a simple servant of the Fourth Estate, devoted to the principles of liberty and democracy, the values of the Enlightenment and the primacy of truth.

Wolf's training was in development economics, with a specialization in international trade. He has described his background in the prefaces to several of his books. Born in London in 1946, he is the son of Jewish refugees from Nazi Europe. His father, Edmund Wolf, was born in Galicia and began his career as a playwright in Vienna; a staunchly anti-communist social democrat, he fled to England in 1937 and later worked as a writer and broadcaster, a leading figure at the BBC's German service and contributor to *Die Zeit*. Wolf's mother was the daughter of a Dutch-Jewish fish merchant who escaped with his family across the North Sea in May 1940, just ahead of the Nazi invasion. Wolf attended UCS, an independent boys' school in Hampstead, and in 1965 went up to Oxford to study classics at Corpus Christi, later switching to PPE. Wolf has repeatedly said that he took his parents' values as his own and never felt the slightest inclination to rebel. At Oxford he became a right-wing member of the Labour Club, inoculated by his father's views against the 'infantile leftism' he encountered there. As he explained in the preface to *Why Globalization Works* (2004), he already knew that 'all the varieties of Marxism were both wicked and stupid', their ideas 'almost as insane as those of the Nazis'. In his view, moderate conservatives, liberals and social democrats were aligned in all the great battles against 'religious fanatics, obscurantists, extreme environmentalists, fascists, Marxists and, of course, contemporary anti-globalizers.'

Politically and intellectually, the turning point for Wolf seems to have been his MPhil in economics at Nuffield, which introduced him to the circle around the development economist Ian Little, an early and influential advocate of trade liberalization. Well-known in World Bank and OECD circles, with a special interest in India, Little was conducting a sustained assault on the prevailing 'structuralist' development orthodoxy with great intellectual brio. This cemented Wolf's conversion from social democracy to 'classical liberalism', while the Fabian Society's rejection of his pamphlet attacking council housing and rent controls snapped his links with Labour. Wolf joined the World Bank in 1971. A young warrior for the open-markets cause, he was assigned first to the East Africa desk and then to India, where he formed lasting friendships and produced a book on the country's (lack of) exports. By the end of the decade, however, he had decided that World Bank lending under Robert McNamara was irredeemably flawed—a Stalinist vision of development, as he put it in *Why Globalization Works*. He relocated to a London think tank, the Trade Policy Research Centre, where, as director of studies, he was free to promote the neoliberal agenda. Thence, after a few tersely written comment pieces for the *Financial Times*, he was recruited as a leader writer on economics for the paper in 1987, becoming chief economics commentator nine years later.

When he joined it, the *Financial Times* was far more highbrow than it has since become, with serious arts criticism and a haughty disdain for the consumerist bling that now crowds its pages. Economics commentary was dominated by the outsize figure of Samuel Brittan, ten years Wolf's senior; a florid stylist and avidly free-market. By comparison, Wolf's pieces were data-heavy and technocratic, almost Fabian; but all the more authoritative for that.

Under its latest editor, Roula Khalaf, an impressive diversity of genders and skin tones among the FT's writers has been matched by an iron conformity in outlook. Khalaf has purged the maverick thinkers who once enlivened its opinion pages; critical voices, notably the acerbic Wolfgang Münchau, have been silenced and former youthful gadflies—Janan Ganesh, as in his time Gideon Rachman—spend most of their wordage hymning the virtues of the West. But if the FT has lost its way, the same could not be said of Wolf.

His latest book extends and deepens a trajectory already indicated by its predecessors. *Why Globalization Works* may have boldly declared that the problem was not too much but too little globalization, but the arc of Wolf's prognoses has pointed down since then. *Fixing Global Finance*, drafted in 2006 though published in 2009, noted that the financial crises brought about by globalization were 'frighteningly expensive' in terms of the victims' shattered lives, even if Wolf did not then foresee the looming meltdown of 2008. Acknowledging this in his next book, *The Shifts and the Shocks* (2014), he worried that 'the financially driven capitalism that emerged from the market-oriented counter revolution has proved too much of a good thing'— liberalization had brought forth a monster, a financial sector capable of devouring its economy. Now, with *The Crisis of Democratic Capitalism*, Wolf notes that he is circling back to the Fabianism of his youth. The last forty years have vindicated Polanyi's claim that humans would not long tolerate a truly free-market system, he argues, and Keynes's concerns have once again become our own.

In this, of course, Wolf joins a growing chorus. Neoliberalism, it turns out, has led to growing income inequality, macro-economic instability and low investment. The economy has been on life support, the political mainstream subjected to serial electoral blows. This ground has been well trodden already by repentant neoliberal writers, among them DeLong and Summers, joined from the centre left by Tooze and Piketty, and from the right by Lind and Zingales—not to mention more radical writers like Streeck, Durand and Brenner. What does *The Crisis of Democratic Capitalism* bring to this already crowded field?

Wolf's diagnosis is apodictic. 'Ruling elites' have been discredited by the economic calamities generated by liberalized finance, compounded by their own moral and intellectual failings. Trump's America and Brexit Britain have blighted liberal democracy in its heartlands. The rise of China has shaken confidence in—and the confidence *of*—the West. The balance between politics and the economy has been broken, Wolf writes: 'We are no longer able to combine the operations of the market economy with stable liberal democracy.' The West must find a new equilibrium between the two, which both depend upon each other. Why is this the case? Wolf sets himself the challenge of explaining their changing relationship. *The Crisis of Democratic*

Capitalism opens with some theoretical and historical scene-setting. Theory here, however, does not involve consideration of other thinkers' systematizations of the problem but a metaphorical fable spun by Wolf himself, in which the economic and the political are anthropomorphized as 'symbiotic twins': economics—producing the means for human subsistence—provides the principal rationale for social cooperation; politics provides the framework within which that cooperation works. During the long millennia of hunter-gatherer bands, cooperation was structured through familial relations; under the ancient agrarian empires, by hierarchy and coercion.

With the emergence of fully monetized economies, however, markets made possible a reduction in the self-sufficiency of households, thereby encouraging specialization and creating ever greater market demand. Market expansion in turn made forced labour—serfdom and slavery—increasingly redundant. An economy that rewarded new commercial ideas brought about a transformation in prosperity. Over the past two centuries, decentralized competition and political consent have become the rule—initiating the 'difficult marriage' of capitalism and democracy. Wolf's theoretical account supplies five reasons for this. First, ideology: both embrace the same underlying values, individual freedom and equality of status. Second, the aspirations of a rising middle class, demanding a voice for itself in social and political life; at the same time, US states began to drop property requirements for the vote and censitary suffrage came to appear 'ridiculous'. Third, the 'organized working class' produced by capitalism pushed for the expansion of democracy. Fourth, elite self-interest: national mobilizations for industrial warfare accelerated the shift towards universal suffrage, especially in a country like Britain where a powerful conservative party could represent the needs of property holders under democratic conditions. Finally, great-power influence: the ruling states of the nineteenth and twentieth centuries, the UK and US, were both 'liberal societies' which could impose their paradigm elsewhere, including through military occupation of Germany and Japan after 1945, though regrettably not on post-Soviet Russia. Yet the marriage—or 'fusion'—that produced democratic capitalism has been fragile. An elected government may try to capture the economy, resulting in socialism, the route to disaster; or, contrariwise, those who control the economy may capture the state, resulting in plutocracy. Democracy thus needs to be protected from capitalism, and capitalism from democracy, by a bulwark of institutions, laws and norms.

Wolf's historical account provides a shift in perspective, pointing out that democratic capitalism is a relatively recent development, dating in his view to around 1870. He catalogues democracy's advances and retreats. In 1900, twelve states counted as democratic, though without universal suffrage; their number rose to 24 in 1922, fell to 9 in 1940, rose again to 18 in 1946,

then swelled to 48 in 1989, with the overthrow of the Latin American dic-
tatorships, and to 97 by 2016, with the democratization of much of the
ex-Soviet bloc, Southeast Asia and Africa. However, the last thirty years have
also seen a 'democratic recession', tracked by the DC-based Freedom House
and political sociologists such as Stanford's Larry Diamond. In the established democracies, voter turnout, party allegiance and trust in parliament
went into decline, with younger cohorts especially disenchanted, while the
non-democracies became increasingly authoritarian. The culmination of
this trend was the election of Trump, whose 'hostility to democratic allies
and democratic norms' and 'contempt for the liberal global economic order'
Wolf regards as potentially transformative.

The Crisis of Democratic Capitalism proposes a rough correlation of
democracy's ups and downs with cycles of economic *laissez faire* versus state
intervention and globalization versus protectionism. Wolf notes that even
before universal suffrage had taken root, the rise of limited liability holdings had produced corporate and financial behemoths. Yet states also grew
more powerful as economic actors, government spending as a percentage
of GDP quadrupling in the advanced economies between 1914 and 1980. In
his telling, the statist turn initiated by the war economies of 1914–18 was
consolidated by distrust of capitalist self-regulation after the 1929 Crash
and Great Depression. The Keynesian consensus held till the 1970s, when
interventionism in turn was discredited by high inflation and unemploy-
ment, combined with weak profitability, slow productivity growth and the
poor performance of nationalized industries. With the Reagan/Thatcher
counter-revolution came a partial return to *laissez faire* through deregulation
of finance, tax cuts and privatization, though state spending remained high.
This new regime in turn began to unravel with what Wolf justly terms the
2007–12 transatlantic financial crisis, requiring state bailouts, re-regulation
and a super-expansionary monetary policy, pioneered in Japan; by the end of
the decade, the 'active state' had returned.

Wolf's rounds of globalization and retrenchment roughly track these
cycles. The first globalization of 1870–1914, contemporaneous with the
advent of democratic capitalism and partial broadenings of suffrage,
involved the export of manufactured goods from the imperial metropo-
lises and of raw materials from the colonies and semi-colonies, aided by
large-scale overseas investment; by 1914, foreign-held assets—mainly Euro-
American holdings in Southern mines and railways—amounted to 19 per
cent of world output. In the major economies, the profits of imperialism
shored up a relative rise in industrial wages and labour protection. The era
of statist macro-economics and the uneven retreat of democracy was then
matched by tariffs and capital controls. The composition of the second era
of globalization, 1980–2012, was quite different to the first: manufacturing

REVIEWS

was 'unbundled', with production chains spread out to benefit from cheap labour costs across the world, coordinated by a few US mega-corporations and retail giants that no longer shared a common national interest with their domestic working class, which in turn were hit much harder and more enduringly than expected by the fall in manufacturing jobs and decline of trade unions. The direction of investment was also reversed, now flowing from the poorer countries, especially China, into financial assets in the rich West, temporarily resolving the problem of structurally deficient demand with the leveraged lending boom that collapsed in 2007–12.

The Crisis of Democratic Capitalism does not suggest a direct causal link between de-globalization and the present 'democratic recession', though Wolf argues that market liberalization generally signals an era of optimism, making democratic politics less conflictual, while trade retrenchment usually coincides with periods of tension, fear and anger. Instead, he draws the lesson that globalization itself is not to blame for democracy's problems. If the underlying causes of the 2007–12 crisis were 'huge (and insufficiently understood) shifts in the world economy', they were transmitted via 'a grossly undercapitalized and under-regulated financial system', and its fallout could have been managed differently. The regionally concentrated impact of the 'China shock' upon industrial America—2 million jobs lost, with minimum social support—made it particularly severe; but this was only one aspect in a larger process of slowdown: weak income growth, low social mobility and rising household debt for middle and lower earners, compounded by growing inequality, driven primarily by huge gains at the top of the distribution, declining male labour-force participation rates and a broader loss of good jobs. This 'hollowing out of the middle classes'—the 'middle element' that Aristotle considered the foundation of a strong and well-run state—explains the erosion of public trust in democratic institutions.

Shifting perspective once again, Wolf pins the blame for this economic malaise not on 1980s liberalization itself but on the domestic institutional forms it took. The root of corruption was the Friedmanite shareholder-value agenda, which led to a profound shift in the aims of the firm: distorting incentives towards leverage and short-termism, it encouraged investors to act as rent-seeking asset-strippers, drove agglomeration and financialization, and ultimately ushered in a globalized rentier capitalism. This central chapter, 'Rise of Rentier Capitalism', is the analytic hinge of the book, offering an explanation for the developments documented since 1980—above all 'the tendency of the powerful to rig the economic and political systems against the rest of society'. The expanding financial sector became 'a vehicle for rent extraction' rather than productive improvements, generating over 20 per cent of total corporate profits, not least by leveraging to hedge against the volatility it had stoked; in Q1 2021, the gross market value of derivatives was over \$12 trillion. Agglomeration and winner-takes-all markets allowed the most successful businesses to dominate swathes of the globe and generate massive monopoly rents. In socio-geographic terms, this produced a few booming metropolitan clusters and thousands of declining provincial towns. The monopsony power of firms in labour markets and 'undue' protection of intellectual property shielded the decline in competition. Large firms have become specialists in exploiting loopholes for tax evasion, while benefiting from the state's provision of public goods and externalizing costs, including onto workers.

The hope that democratic processes might regulate firms to offset these processes 'assumes a neutral political process in which well-intentioned legislatures respond to the choices of well-informed voters', Wolf writes. 'Nothing could be further from reality.' It is all too easy for large firms to buy the political and regulatory protection they desire; Congressmen, he notes, spend thirty hours a week raising money. The financial sector has become increasingly dependent on political backing: 'That profits have remained so high subsequent to the crisis must be due in large part to the immense support provided by the authorities, especially the near-zero interest rates that have been in effect for so much of the time, as well as the still gigantic balance sheets of financial institutions.' Rather than being exemplars of 'duty, fairness, responsibility and decency', the erosion of elite moral standards is such that these bankers now see themselves as involved in a status game. This scale of rent extraction and maldistribution—far greater than could have been imagined in 1980—has left a large part of the population 'confused, frustrated and angry'.

All this led to a dangerous populist reaction. But Western democratic capitalisms are now threatened externally as well by two other variants: 'demagogic authoritarian capitalism', or DAC, of the sort that has emerged in Turkey, the Philippines, Poland, Russia and Hungary—which they might become; and 'bureaucratic authoritarian capitalism', or BAC, the type that has developed in China and Vietnam, which might defeat them. In this context, Wolf now regrets the 1980s weakening of trade unions and hollowing of traditional parties. He endorses Martin Baxter's claim that contemporary politics has shifted from being a one-dimensional struggle fought on economic issues—counter-posing a centre right, backed by business, the professional middle class and the self-employed, to a centre left, based in the industrial working class—to a three-dimensional struggle, in which conflicts occur in the economic, social and national dimensions. This, argues Wolf, makes politics more identity based, with a 'Brahmin Left', as Piketty terms it, now opposed to a 'Merchant Right' and an atomized working-class remnant.

The task therefore is to save both liberal democracy and global capitalism together. Wolf's beacon here is Karl Popper and his concept of 'piecemeal engineering'. This requires 'expertise', but there is also an important role for 'public engagement', both to help formulate goals and to elicit consent from the masses for carrying them through. Renewing capitalism requires, first, a rising standard of living, which in turn will need a substantial level of 'high-quality investment'—to be spurred by income redistribution, negative deposit and lending rates as incentives for private investment; direct monetary transfers from the central bank to the government and a combination of 'tax cuts and higher spending, especially on public investment'. A series of local and national investment banks could help to provide good jobs ('for those prepared to work'). Better education—and 'special opportunities for exceptional children'—will help promote equality of opportunity. The welfare state, suggests Wolf, should be 'rounded out' to provide health, old-age and accident insurance, but 'should not encourage idleness or fecklessness'. Finally, reversing the shareholder-value revolution, reining in executive pay, pursuing anti-monopoly policies and regulating algorithms in the tech sector will help to end 'special privileges for the few'.

Wolf also endorses constitutional reform. Bi-cameral legislatures should be replaced with tri-cameral ones: an elected House of Representatives would produce the government and initiate legislation, on the model of the House of Commons; an appointed House of Merit, consisting of 'people of exceptional achievement in a wide range of civic activities', could delay and amend representation, like a reformed House of Lords. The third, a House of the People whose members would be chosen by sortition, could 'delay legislation' and 'consider controversial questions', but otherwise would be powerless. Democracy cannot work without robust safeguards, of which the most important are not the words of a constitution, which can be politicized and subverted, but 'the hearts and minds of the people, and especially of the elites.' The book ends with an appeal to the latter:

> Members of a functioning elite, which includes the business elite, need wisdom as well as knowledge. Above all, they need to feel responsible for the welfare of their republic and its citizens. Indeed, if there are to be citizens at all, members of the elite must be exemplars. It is not hard: instead of lies, honesty; instead of greed, restraint; instead of fear and hatred, appeals to what Abraham Lincoln called 'the better angels of our nature'.

What to make of all this? First, it is important to understand that *The Crisis of Democratic Capitalism* is a pedagogical text: a sort of mirror for princes, held up to the 'elites'—a 'we' constantly addressed but never specified. Wolf marshals a considerable amount of evidence to shame this collective pronoun into rectifying its bad behaviour and embracing 'reasonableness'. Thus, the international monetary system needs to handle cross-border capital flows in 'a reasonably safe manner'; 'what is needed is a reasonably complete system of social protection'; 'why people of immeasurable wealth should fight so hard not to pay taxes is beyond the understanding of any reasonable person'; 'it is reasonable to be of two minds on the advisability of tax deductibility of gifts'; 'there is no obvious reason why all these rents should accrue to the shareholders and top managers.' Wolf never says what a 'reasonable' level of safety, a 'reasonable' amount of social protection, a 'reasonable' understanding of tax evasion or gift deductibility, or a 'reasonable' degree of rent extraction might be. It is clear, however, that 'reason' in this context refers to something different and thicker than what might be considered merely 'rational'. The standard here is more Burkean, something like a pre-existent, self-evident but unarticulated consensus. (This pedagogical imperative helps to explain the puzzle of Wolf's strained metaphor of the symbiotic twins' marriage, compounded in his historical account of one twin giving birth to the other. Why should such a capable thinker indulge in such conceptual confusion? The mystery is solved once we think of it as a figure in an after-dinner speech to well-banqueted asset-fund managers.)

With this ideal audience in mind, let's turn to the analytic challenge of the book. Its ambition, to relate the etiolation of democratic politics in the rich world to the lopsided development of capitalism, protects Wolf against weak culturalist explanations resting on the putative racism or xenophobia of the mass of the population. As he rightly stresses, the crucial difficulty with primarily cultural explanations is that they fail to answer the obvious question: why now? Does Wolf's analysis, however, explain what is happening any better? We might begin by asking how he understands his key terms, capitalism and democracy. The first is referenced by a cluster of concepts: 'capitalism', 'market capitalism', 'democratic capitalism', 'predatory capitalism', 'competitive capitalism' and 'rentier capitalism', as well as DAC and BAC. To begin with, capitalism for Wolf is 'an economy in which markets, competition, private economic initiative and private property play central roles'. What is striking is how generic and unworkable this is as a tool for identifying any specific economic form. For of course competition, private economic initiative and markets played 'central roles' in both classical antiquity and the medieval world, without thereby leading to anything like economic growth. In particular, market expansion of itself has nowhere led 'forced labour' to become 'increasingly redundant'. It is enough to recall how the linking of Tsarist Russia, East Elbian Germany and the US Cotton South into global agriculture markets reinforced harsh labour regimes in each case. As Maurice Dobb put it: a concept of capitalism as primarily a *commercial* system is insufficiently restrictive to confine the term to any one epoch of economic history. Quite logically, given the conceptual vagueness of Wolf's implicitly commercial model, his attempt to periodize capitalism and create sub-varieties within it remains opaque.

This is particularly true of the key notion of 'rentier capitalism', which is nowhere explicitly conceptualized. Wolf instead offers descriptive tags, such as: 'the tendency of the powerful to rig the economic and political systems against the rest of society', 'the exploitation of market and political power to achieve returns over the market price', 'rigged capitalism' or simply 'plutocracy'. The problem again is that all of these could apply to virtually any phase of any capitalist society, and to many pre-capitalist ones as well. Is there any social order where the powerful do not tend to 'rig' the economic and political system? Where have capitalists *not* exploited 'market and political power'? What is 'unrigged' as opposed to 'rigged' capitalism? How does 'plutocracy' define a phase of capitalism, or even any specific form of class society? Wolf's more detailed analysis of the new economy makes little headway. Financialization is a relatively new phenomenon, although Wolf does not explain where it came from. But the other features that Wolf attributes to rentier capitalism—agglomeration, monopsony, uneven development, tax evasion, cost externalization and a general 'erosion of ethical standards' are entirely non-specific. Although Wolf claims that 'profit is not a good motivating goal for organizations', the orientation toward profit has surely been the defining feature of capitalist firms since their beginning. The shareholder-value agenda seems to identify a more historically specific change, but it was championed at the time as a return to basics. The drive to internalize gains while externalizing losses similarly describes a straightforward capitalist *modus operandi*.

This non-specificity becomes critical when it comes to explaining the slowdown in growth itself, which for Wolf is a key to the crisis of democracy (and rightly belongs at the centre of any explanation). To his credit, Wolf fully acknowledges the problem. 'There is little sign', he writes, 'of the sorts of innovations that would generate an explosion in high-wage, rent-sharing jobs for less-skilled people.' But why is this so? What tendency has found expression in structural stagnation? Wolf has no answer, in part, one suspects, because he has no adequate analysis of what distinguishes the current phase of 'rentier capitalism', or, as I have suggested, even capitalism as such, from what came before. The 'decline in productivity growth is deep and structural', we are told. 'The dynamic capitalist economy of old has just become elderly.' Such non-explanations, or empty but explanatory-sounding phrases, proliferate throughout the chapter on rentier capitalism, reaching their apogée with the following passage:

> Thus the underlying problems have tended to become worse over time, not better. They are deep-seated, reflecting, as they do, macroeconomic imbalances that are themselves the result of global economic integration, the rise of China, the emergence of a globalized form of rentier capitalism and increases in income inequality.

These words mask a muddle. What 'macroeconomic imbalances', and how are these the result of 'economic integration'? How does globalized rentier capitalism differ from non-globalized rentier capitalism? Should we be focused on globalization or rentier capitalism (even if we could be clear about what this latter term means)? Wolf remains silent about what the underlying deep-seated problems are. Furthermore, the statement appears to exist in a strange world in which an unnamed noumenal 'structure' exists *atop* phenomena that it 'reflects': a Kantianism planted firmly on its head. Who could navigate this hall of mirrors?

We run into a different set of problems with democracy, or more precisely 'liberal democracy'. For Wolf, this is defined as a system with 'free and fair elections; active participation of people, as citizens, in civic life; protection of the civil and human rights of all citizens equally; and a rule of law that binds all citizens equally'. This is of course a common enough description, particularly among anglophone political scientists. The conceptual problem here is not that the notion is too generic; rather, it is that it combines a variety of things which either have little internal relationship, or are in active opposition to one another. Wolf, like many liberal thinkers, tries to neutralize these tensions by constructing an abstract descriptive checklist. But this fails. Few would argue for 'rigged and unfair' elections, but are 'free and fair' ones intrinsically democratic? Only according to the dogma that equates a *method* (elections) with the *goal* (the rule of the people). The Greeks of course associated elections with oligarchic rule; only rule by lot was democratic. Is 'free and active participation of the citizens in civic life' necessarily compatible with respect for rights and the rule of law? Such participation, think of the events of January 6 in the US, can be both free and active, but oriented against the law, and against rights. More generally isn't the rule of law as a set of principles that 'binds all citizens equally' a quite undemocratic idea? Surely the democratic method is one in which the people are unbound by any such hypostatized institution?

Wolf's conglomerate understanding of democracy as 'liberal democracy' leads to further problems for his attempt to specify the connections between it and capitalism. He claims, in the first place, that democracy and capitalism rest on common 'underlying values', equality of status and individual freedom. But equality of status—the post-feudal condition that Tocqueville identified in 1830s America, but also regarded with substantial scepticism— is a sociological category, not a principle, while individual freedom is not a democratic value but a liberal one. John Stuart Mill was famously sceptical about the extension of suffrage to the working class, precisely because of the potential threat that this posed to the liberty of property holders. For the giants of nineteenth-century liberalism, censitary suffrage was not, as Wolf would have it, 'transparently ridiculous'. It was understood in that tradition as a central means of protecting individual freedom against the threat of those without property and the tyranny of religious dogmatism. It is no accident that no nineteenth-century liberal did as much for the cause of universal suffrage as those two very illiberal figures, Napoleon III and Bismarck.

Wolf's further arguments about the connection between capitalism and democracy are weak for the opposite reason. He claims that some combination of a rising standard of living and the emergence of the working class, both caused by capitalism, led people to express a desire for a 'voice'. The problem with this argument is that, although the nineteenth century saw many movements for the expansion of political rights, they were by no means universally supportive of liberalism, especially where they were most closely associated with the emerging capitalist class structure. The notion that the organized working class was a champion of *liberal* democracy is barely true even for the British case, where working-class representatives were actually incorporated as a junior wing of the Liberal Party. The most organized working classes—in *belle époque* Italy and Germany for example—aimed to establish socialist democracy, conceived as a political order beyond liberalism. In the US, which Wolf describes repeatedly as the world's most important democracy, organized workers as such have had virtually no impact on the political order. The key social force for democratic expansion in the nineteenth century was the farm population (as was also true in a different way for France).

Wolf's conceptual and terminological ambiguity here serves to mask the fact that he is mostly concerned not with the fate of democracy, but rather with defending a particular brand of liberalism. This is most obvious in the minimal reforms he proposes; the mountain of democratic-capitalist crisis gives birth to a mouse. Most of his prescriptions for 'renewing capitalism'—promoting investment, NIBS, a slimline welfare state—are already in operation, including green and diversity-sensitive revisions to the shareholder agenda. 'Renewing democracy' is in favour of fair voting, but Wolf's emphasis falls on 'professional politics, disinterested expertise, independent institutions'. His sanitized House of Merit is clearly an anti-democratic institution on any natural understanding of that latter term. Surprising too, from the point of view of democracy, is Wolf's embrace of the principle of 'subsidiarity'. The author praises a handful of small rich countries, Denmark of course leading the list, for being able to 'combine the benefits of *global scale* in business operations with those of *small scale* in politics'. But 'governance also needs to be transferred upward if states are to serve the interests of their people'. Effectively this presents one of the key elements of the contemporary crisis of democracy, the hollowing out both from above and from below of what Streeck has termed the small and mid-sized European nation states, as a political ideal. In this Wolf exemplifies a common trait of liberal commentary on the contemporary moment: the uncritical embrace of those very features of the political order that have caused the hated 'populist reaction'.

Finally, it is worth dwelling for a moment on the gulf between the analytic sections of the book and its programme of elite pedagogy, rooted in the 'reasonableness' of the upper crust. The reader is first told that the 'problems are deep and structural', that the historical phase of the welfare state has passed and that the marriage of capitalism and democracy was late and difficult. But Wolf's political prescription says that solutions are 'not hard' and that the programme should be essentially a modernized version of the mid-century settlement. Stranger still, Wolf's conclusion attributes the crisis of democracy in part to 'elite failures and malfeasance' and explains Trump and Brexit as the result of 'forty years of elite failure'. But as even the most casual reader of Piketty would be aware, the 'elites' have succeeded stupendously over this period. To admit that, of course, would suggest a political solution beyond civic lessons for the ruling bloc. It points to the need for a popular subjectivity, which in Wolf's universe is one of the main threats to 'liberal democracy'. Whatever else one might say about the current period, the political nature of the distribution of social and economic power has never been more obvious. To leave these questions in the hands of 'policy makers' and 'disinterested experts' would represent not democracy's resurgence, but rather its defeat.

independent thinking from polity

The Common
Antonio Negri
Translated by Ed Emery

This final volume in Antonio Negri's new trilogy aims to clarify and develop the 'common' as a key concept of radical thought. Here the 'common' is understood in a double sense: on the one hand, as a collective of production and consumption in which the domination of capital has been completely realized; on the other hand, as the cooperation of workers and citizens and their assertion of political power.

Like its companion volumes, this new collection of essays by Negri will be a valuable resource for anyone interested in radical politics and in the key social and political struggles of our time.

PB 978-1-5095-4427-1 | June 2023 | £15.99

Cancelled
The Left Way Back from Woke
Umut Özkırımlı

In this provocative book, Umut Özkırımlı reveals how the Left has been sucked into a spiral of toxic hatred and outrage-mongering, retreating from the democratic ideals of freedom, tolerance and pluralism that it purports to represent. Exploring the similarities between right-wing populism and radical identity politics, he sets out an alternative vision. It is only by focusing on our common humanity and working across differences that the Left will successfully find a constructive and consensual way back from "woke".

PB: 978-1-5095-5092-0 | March 2023 | £14.99

Taking Control
Sovereignty and Democracy After Brexit
Philip Cunliffe, George Hoare, Lee Jones, Peter Ramsay

This book makes the democratic case for national sovereignty, arguing for a radical, forward-looking reconstitution of the British nation-state through strengthening representative democracy. It is essential for anyone who wonders why British politics is so dysfunctional and who wants to do better.

PB: 978-1-5095-5320-4 | April 2023 | £15.99

The Culture of Stopping
Harald Welzer
Translated by Sharon Howe

Our culture has no concept of stopping. We continue to build motorways and airports for a future in which cars and planes may no longer exist. We're converting our planet from a natural one to an artificial one in which the quantity of man-made objects now exceeds the totality of living matter. We're on a treadmill to disaster.

HB: 978-1-5095-5587-1 | June 2023 | £20.00

Go to **www.politybooks.com** to order   @politybooks   facebook.com/politybooks

Peter Dews, *Schelling's Late Philosophy in Confrontation with Hegel*
Oxford University Press: New York 2023
311 pp, 978 0 19 006912 4

CHRISTOPH SCHURINGA

SCHELLING'S CHALLENGE

The work of Hegel has undergone a remarkable process of domestication by Anglo-Saxon philosophers over the past thirty years. Hegel is no longer the ambitious metaphysician he had always seemed to be—and as he was still portrayed by the Canadian philosopher Charles Taylor in his monumental *Hegel* (1975). With an initial impetus from Robert Pippin's *Hegel's Idealism* (1989), analytic philosophers laboured to make the German thinker safe for the academic establishment of the English-speaking world by essentially presenting him as a radicalizer of Kant. Just as Kant's critical project was not itself a metaphysical theory, but an enquiry into the conditions of possibility of metaphysics, so Hegel was now seen as a thinker who merely tightened the screws on Kant's project of delineating the general thought-structures that render metaphysics possible. In this view, Hegel was no longer the cautious political philosopher who, as he puts it in the Preface to his *Philosophy of Right*, restricts himself to painting philosophy's retrospective 'grey on grey', once a shape of life has 'grown old'. Instead he emerged as a radical social critic, advocating a programme for the overthrow of capitalism that strongly anticipates that of Marx. In a startling twist, this approach has recently found its way back to Germany, and is manifested in the work of what remains of the Frankfurt School of critical theory.

This recasting of Hegel makes him only a little more ambitious than Kant in the realm of metaphysics and, equally remarkably, only a little less so than Marx in the realm of social thought—in spite of Marx's own understanding of himself as a radical critic of Hegel. One serious consequence of this reinterpretation is that Hegel's relationship to his contemporary

Schelling starts to become illegible. Indeed Schelling, in this light, looks so *outré* that he can be treated only as an aberrant deviation from the true path leading from Kant to Hegel. To understand how the rehabilitated Hegel serves to obscure the relationship with Schelling, we might start by rehearsing the famous early episodes of their shared intellectual biography.

When Schelling came to study at the Protestant Seminary in Tübingen in 1790, at the precocious age of fifteen, he not only shared lodgings with Hegel and Hölderlin, themselves just twenty, but formed with his two older contemporaries an inextricably joint intellectual life. The explosive events of the French Revolution had detonated a matching ferment of ideas in Germany, where Kant's 'revolution in philosophy' had just unleashed a new set of questions concerning the unity and reach of reason. The contributions of each of the trio to the intensely ambitious and systematizing philosophical activity that became known as German Idealism cannot now be untangled, but it is clear that Schelling, despite his youth, was from early on the driving force. Both Schelling and Hegel left unsigned the texts they each contributed to a new review that they co-produced, the *Critical Journal of Philosophy* (1802–3). Hegel's first important philosophical text, *The Difference Between Fichte's and Schelling's System of Philosophy* (1801), firmly took the side of Schelling against that of Fichte. Schelling had by this time produced a series of works setting out the various fluctuating versions of his philosophical system, and of the 'philosophy of nature' that was a crucial component of it, publishing his *System of Transcendental Idealism* in 1800.

Hegel was slower than his *Wunderkind* friend to reach philosophical maturity. As he came to reject Schelling's 'identity philosophy', he caused an unhealable rift between the two, cauterized in remarks he directed at Schelling in his first philosophical masterpiece, *The Phenomenology of Spirit* (1807). Once installed as professor of philosophy in Berlin in 1818, Hegel began to portray himself as not only the culmination of German Idealism—the apex of a triad of which Fichte and Schelling were supporting elements—but of philosophy as such. While Hegel's alleged 'accommodation' to the increasingly conservative political circumstances prevailing in Prussia may be debated, he was unequivocal that further progress beyond him in philosophy was not to be countenanced, with his system set out in complete and cast-iron form in his *Encyclopaedia of the Philosophical Sciences*, first published in 1817. Only after Hegel's sudden death at the height of his powers in 1831 did Schelling have a chance to offer a philosophical reply to his former friend. In 1841 he was called to a professorship in Berlin with the instruction to 'stamp out the dragon seed' of Hegelianism. His inaugural lecture course was attended by Friedrich Engels, Søren Kierkegaard, Mikhail Bakunin, Jacob Burckhardt and Leopold von Ranke. Whether or not

Schelling effected the hoped-for restoration in political terms, the scene was indeed set for a confrontation with Hegel's legacy.

This familiar narrative is difficult to make sense of in light of the rehabilitated Hegel, standing in a line from Kant whose only intermediate station is Fichte—with Schelling appearing as an embarrassing and even shocking deviation. Never fitting easily into the story of German Idealism, Schelling's critique of Hegel seems, on this reading, like mere reaction, in two senses of the word. Schelling is merely reactive, in that he simply responds to Hegel's already formed philosophy—as opposed to renegotiating on his own terms an intellectual project of which he had been an original progenitor. And this reactiveness is explained by reaction in an ideological sense—Schelling's tendency to theological bloviation and predilection for the mythological. Reflection on the joint intellectual trajectory that Hegel and Schelling pursued, in utmost earnestness, before they went their separate ways, helps to render this picture implausible. A decisive demonstration of this implausibility requires, however, a detailed co-examination of both Hegel and Schelling.

Such a detailed philosophical examination is what Peter Dews offers in *Schelling's Late Philosophy in Confrontation with Hegel*, the distillation of decades of scholarly and philosophical work. Dews does not limit the book to an analysis of the late Schelling's critique of Hegel—something for which Anglophone precedents exist. Instead, he compares Hegel's thought with Schelling's late philosophy 'along a broad front', in the service of mounting a defence of Schelling. In doing so, he draws deeply on the work of German scholars such as Michael Theunissen and Manfred Frank, still underappreciated by Anglophone interpreters. Dews's approach allows him to illuminate the challenge that Schelling poses to Hegel, a challenge that the rehabilitated version renders invisible. An appreciation of Schelling's profound understanding of his former friend and colleague's project allows us to read him as striking at that system's root.

Schelling's Late Philosophy is a work in three parts. The opening chapters trace the complex evolution of Schelling's early work, from the debate with Fichte to his elaboration of freedom in the *Freiheitsschrift*. A constant through this early work is Schelling's insistence that philosophy is bipartite, and that its two parts, transcendental philosophy and the philosophy of nature, stand on an equal footing. Schelling changes his mind over time, however, on the status of these two parts relative to each other—are they coextensive, or do they mutually require each other as complements? For a period, he pursues a Spinozistic 'identity philosophy', according to which they are coeval and equipollent. The central section of the book takes us into Schelling's late philosophy. Dews's principal aim here is to delineate the two philosophical strands that Schelling calls 'negative philosophy' and 'positive philosophy'. Although the respective roles of these strands might loosely be compared to those of Hegel's logic and *Realphilosophie*—his philosophy of the 'real' which covers nature and spirit, in turn—it is important that, on the whole, the distinction is a different one. 'Negative philosophy' is an *a priori* science, and in that sense like Hegel's logic, but it is not a theory of 'thought-determinations' that form a self-contained whole. It is a theory of 'types of entity', and so of what there *can* be. 'Positive philosophy', for its part, has nothing to do with positivism, or even with the idea of 'starting from the positive'—that is, of what is given to the senses—as conceived of, for instance, by Feuerbach. Beginning from a hypothesis produced by negative philosophy as it encounters its limit, positive philosophy engages in a hermeneutics of the history of human consciousness. Positive philosophy could be characterized as empirical, with the stricture that its basis is an experience of the sheer facticity of the world—what Schelling calls 'unpre-thinkable being'. The final section of Dews's book sets out the general tendency of positive philosophy, concerned largely with the transition from mythological consciousness to revelation, and from there to what Schelling calls 'philosophical religion'.

The opening chapters of *Schelling's Late Philosophy* are important in that they substantiate the way in which Schelling's development emerges out of a joint trajectory with Hegel, as well as helping to illuminate the complex development of Schelling's own divergent path. But what is most striking here is Dews's treatment of the late philosophy as it develops from this earlier period. While in his youthful work Schelling had experimented with various versions of a two-part philosophy, from the moment of his Munich *System der Weltalter* lectures of 1827–8 on, he operates with a distinction between 'negative' (sometimes also 'purely rational') and 'positive' (sometimes also 'historical') philosophy. We begin with negative philosophy, which we pursue until, in its culmination, it pushes over into positive philosophy.

Negative philosophy is, like Hegel's logic, *a priori*, dialectical, self-moving. It works, as Dews puts it, through a 'progressive, dialectical determination of the fundamental configurations of possible being'. As with Hegel's logic, it begins from pure being as such, but conceived as the pure potentiality that is isolated when all specifications of ways to be are stripped away. Negative (or 'rational') philosophy looks radically distinct from Hegel's logic, however, in that it generates a dialectic not of categories, but of *Potenzen*, a term with connotations of both 'potentiality' and 'power'. Each *Potenz* generates the next, until the culmination of negative philosophy in its thinking of itself, which Schelling—like Hegel—calls the Idea. Unlike Hegel's Idea, however, Schelling's pushes us over into another kind of philosophy.

Positive philosophy is, again, quite distinct from Hegel's *Realphilosophie*. We can see this already by considering that negative philosophy, as a determination of all kinds of things there *can* be, *is* already *Realphilosophie*. Furthermore, positive philosophy is unlike anything Hegel finds a place for in his philosophical system. Positive philosophy is, according to Dews, 'abductive'—that is, it engages in the form of argument also called 'inference to the best explanation'; it seeks to explain human thought, taking as its point of origin the dreamlike structure of mythological consciousness. One implication of this is that, whereas Hegel's *Realphilosophie* must refer back to the logic as its template, positive philosophy does not in this way refer back to negative philosophy, but reaches out into a fundamentally different mode of demonstration.

Tellingly, as Dews shows, Hegel faces a problem of which Schelling is free. Hegel's logic is a self-contained circle of 'thought-determinations'. It culminates in the Idea, the 'accomplished totality of determinations' that closes over its own self-generation. But somehow, despite its own self-completion, the logic must now generate something other out of itself, or somehow give way to another part of philosophy, the *Realphilosophie*. We might here ask with Marx, in the Paris Manuscripts, whether the Idea engages in this act of generation out of 'boredom'. More seriously, we might consider that it remains unclear in what sense the *Realphilosophie* is supposed to be (or could be) heterogeneous with respect to the logic at all, since it seems, no less than the logic, to consist in the conceptual specification of reality. Perhaps it performs this specification in greater detail, but then one wonders why this detail could not have been accommodated in the logic. In fact, the heterogeneity of logic and *Realphilosophie* seems to be important to Hegel: he characterizes the Idea as *noch logisch*, 'still logical', as Dews emphasizes several times, and so standing in need of something no longer logical beyond itself. It would seem then, as Schelling protests in *On the Source of the Eternal Truths*, the final lecture he gave to the Berlin Academy of Sciences in old age, that Hegel's Idea is supposed to 'break apart into this world of contingent things, opaque to reason and resistant to the concept'. It seems to do so, as Schelling says, 'without rhyme or reason' because, logic having closed over itself, it cannot possibly stretch out a *logical* bridge over to the shore of the real.

Schelling's Idea, in which his negative philosophy culminates, functions quite differently from that of Hegel. In one of his most astonishing moves, Schelling seeks to show, by rational means, its non-self-sufficiency. The Idea requires something that exceeds it, which Schelling calls *das reine Daß*—the pure 'that', the sheer facticity of anything's existing at all—as its basis. I say 'basis', since the Idea does not admit of anything, let alone the pure 'that', as a rational *ground*. This basis is 'un-pre-thinkable'. That it can be seen as the basis of the Idea at all can only come into view when it is recognized that, although 'un-pre-thinkable', it is not 'un-post-thinkable'. Post-thinking is what positive philosophy is supposed to accomplish.

Particularly audacious is the way in which Schelling links his putative insight into the necessity of *das reine Daß* as the basis of the Idea to something which he thought Kant had glimpsed in the *Critique of Pure Reason*. As Dews reports, Schelling claimed in his 1842–43 *Grounding of Positive Philosophy* that Kant had reached the threshold of the transition to 'positive philosophy'. Kant's treatment of the 'Ideal of Pure Reason', in which God is the ground of all reality, demonstrated that he was aware—contrary to his own statements—that reason 'demands *more* than it can generate from its own resources alone'. Kant is repelled by the thought of God's 'groundlessly necessary existence' but nonetheless experiences its irresistibility. Schelling invites us to embrace this incomprehensibility as the profound truth that he takes it to be. For God to be what He is, He is required to show up against the background of his own groundlessness. It is here that negative philosophy turns over into positive philosophy. In seeking to understand the actual world, we have to begin from the 'hypothesis', Schelling says, that there has indeed been an inaugural transition from pure blind beingness to intelligibility. Positive philosophy tries to make sense of the course of the world in light of that, and thereby to substantiate it. The contrast with Hegel's self-confirming rationalism could hardly be greater.

The post-thinking that positive philosophy performs takes the form of a hermeneutics of the history of human consciousness—which turns out to be largely the history of religious mythology. This is, of course, one of the most controversial aspects of Schelling's whole undertaking. However, one upshot of Schelling's articulation of a distinct space for religion, as emerging from *das reine Daß*, is that he can claim to overcome a difficulty in Hegel over the relationship between religion and philosophy. For Hegel, art, religion and philosophy are, successively, the three forms of 'absolute spirit', with philosophy the highest of the three. Religion anticipates philosophy, attempting to convey the rational content of philosophy in non-rational form. This leaves the door open to the demand simply to replace religion with philosophy, since philosophy, per Hegel's picture, merely does better what religion attempts to do. Hegel, as a committed Lutheran, was far from wanting to take this step himself. Nevertheless, this possibility was avidly exploited by Left Hegelians after his death.

Schelling's conception of the relationship between religion and philosophy, as Dews presents it, is quite different. Religion, particularly in its 'highest' form, Christianity, is not to be understood as a body of doctrine but as consciousness itself, struggling against all limitation. In this, it is fundamentally distinct from philosophy, so that it could not possibly be the anticipation of philosophy that it is for Hegel. Religion is not to be superseded by philosophy. Rather, both point to the need for 'philosophical religion'. Unfortunately, however, Schelling says that 'philosophical religion, as we demand it, *does not exist*', and as Dews adds, 'this is because it will *always* be to come'.

Whether or not Dews's interpretation and defence of Schelling's projects of negative and positive philosophy is ultimately convincing, there can be no doubt that the book is important for a number of reasons. One is simply that Schelling's late thought is presented with a cogency that is unprecedented in the Anglophone literature. Dews is an unusual figure within contemporary philosophical writing in that he is able to distil the ideas of the most forbidding writers and present them in a disarmingly lucid style, sometimes bordering on the irreverent (Schelling's 'haughty esotericism' is 'admittedly unattractive'; the problem of the thing-in-itself the 'most irritating' of the perplexities generated by Kant). It is almost as if he has sought to make good on the aspirations to precision and clarity that are such a prominent feature of analytic philosophers' self-conception, even though—or precisely because—his own background is not analytic. Unusually, Dews made his way into philosophy from the study of literature, having resolved to understand Derrida from a philosophical, rather than a literary, point of view. Readers familiar with his writings on twentieth-century thought will be aware that this work has often drawn on German Idealism, and Schelling in particular. A striking example is the first chapter of *Logics of Disintegration* (1987), the critique of post-structuralism which established his reputation. Here he identifies in the *early* Schelling a refusal to select one member of the subject–object binary as the absolute beginning of philosophy, and finds echoes of this in Derrida's philosophical ensemble of *différance*, archewriting and the trace, which seek to transcend such binaries by elevating transcendental critique to the level of—in a strikingly Schellingian phrase for Derrida to employ—an 'ultra-transcendental text'. Dews's *The Idea of Evil* (2008) already signalled that his preoccupation with German Idealism would develop in new directions; in this most recent book, he has arrived at the heart of the matter as far as this long-standing interest is concerned.

The challenge that *Schelling's Late Philosophy* poses to the rehabilitated Hegel, something which Dews signals in his Introduction, seems to me both salutary and highly secure. The book leaves no doubt that the attempt to render Hegel 'analytically acceptable' by removing Schelling from the development of German Idealism is eccentric and unsustainable. Dews's book, if obliquely, joins an emerging field of dissent in Anglophone Hegel scholarship, for example the work of James Kreines. A peculiar feature of the Anglo-Saxon domestication of Hegel is that the acceptability it seeks to secure for the most famous of the German Idealists rests on a set of assumptions that were widely held in the 1980s and 1990s, but which are now *passé* in analytic philosophy—those associated with what was called 'naturalism'. (Consensus around the *attractiveness* of 'naturalism' was once widespread, although no one could agree what it was.) One side of the story was that it became commonplace to deny that Hegel espoused a metaphysical conception of human history, and to ridicule as naïve the notion of '*Geist* pulling the strings'. The other was the claim that Hegel advocated a radical social philosophy founded on a merely structural theory of 'recognitive relations' among subjects; a notion that has found its way into German intellectual currents deriving from critical theory, such as the work of Axel Honneth.

Instead, Dews shows Schelling to engage with the nerve of Hegel's thought, its attempt to provide a self-completing philosophy. In this light, Schelling's project, while no less ambitious in aspiration, appears bracingly divergent. Positive philosophy is like nothing dreamt of in Hegel, thanks to the way in which negative philosophy requires the Idea to exceed itself in *das reine Daß*. The idea of philosophy exceeding itself, as it hits a barrier of reality it cannot subsume back into itself, is here made the very principle of philosophy. The radicality of this proposal can hardly be overestimated. How attractive, however, especially in political terms, is what Schelling offers as a response to Hegel's legacy? One might wonder if Schelling's contribution is not, after all, a flight into religion—even if to a church yet to come—that confirms suspicions about the reactionary function of his late thought.

Dews briefly mentions Marx and Kierkegaard as standing for 'two paradigmatic responses to Hegel's enterprise'. In response to Hegel's erasure of the 'distinction between knowledge and the existential dimension of faith', Kierkegaard sought to reinstate the latter, whereas Marx sought to abolish religion altogether. In light of these concrete, though very different, proposals, is Schelling's talk of an unprecedented, and perhaps unrealizable, 'Johannine Church' that will heal the rifts of all previous Christianity more than a mere gesture? Perhaps Schelling is refreshingly open when it comes to the possibilities of the future, in a way that Hegel notoriously struggles to be. But what is there to recommend his vision to us?

Again, we might find it refreshing that Schelling recognizes regress as well as progress in history, but to accommodate this Dews relies on the troublesome notion of 'reflective equilibrium'. He writes that 'in order to evaluate theological developments, to determine what constitutes an enlargement of truth and what represents a regressive occlusion or distortion of it, there is a need to shuttle back and forth between an orientation toward the moment of origin and a focus on the current endpoint, in a process of reflective equilibrium'. The problem with the concept of reflective equilibrium, here as elsewhere, is that it offers an image of stability, but seems only to have shifted the criterion from difficult-to-specify extremes to an equally difficult-to-specify centre point.

It may seem an attractive feature of Schelling's thought, as Dews presents it, that history here is not a story of freedom, as for Hegel, but of liberation. Hegel has the actualization of freedom be guaranteed by the institutions of the state. Schelling can seem less restrictive, with his concept of liberation encompassing the bracing notion of a freedom 'to be free or unfree'. Dews assures us that Schelling's positive philosophy 'has an irreducible future-oriented dimension'. It is portrayed as emancipatory, thanks to its engaging in 'affirmative genealogy' (a phrase Dews borrows from Hans Joas). 'Affirmative genealogy' is unlike what analytic philosophers have called 'vindicatory genealogy'; it is contrasted with 'debunking' genealogy of the Nietzschean kind in *clarifying*, Dews tells us, not in vindicating. Schelling's positive philosophy is rich in proto-psychoanalytic insight into the constitution of our consciousness, as Dews suggests. Be this as it may, it is hard to shake off the question of whether emancipation does not, as the Young Hegelians urged, lie precisely in liberation *from* the religious consciousness whose rich veins it mines.

Dews's book decisively disturbs what has been made of German Idealism in recent years, thanks to the skewed picture of Hegel that has become entrenched in the American sphere of influence (including Germany). His Schelling is philosophically powerful, provocative, fascinating and subtle. As a result, Schelling appears as a philosophical interlocutor of the first importance for Hegel, and Hegelians, to grapple with. Whatever one thinks of Schelling's negative and positive philosophy as Dews portrays them, it is clear that, in the wake of this tremendously lucid presentation, our understanding of German Idealism has received a powerful new impetus.

LEUVEN UNIVERSITY PRESS   www.lup.be - info@lup.be

History of Japanese Art after 1945
Institutions, Discourse, Practice

Kitazawa Noriaki, Kuresawa Takemi, Mitsuda Yuri

€ 45,00 / £41.00 | HB
ISBN 9789462703544
ebook

Anarchy of the Body Undercurrents of
Performance Art in 1960s Japan
KuroDalaiJee

€ 55,00 / £49.00 | HB
ISBN 9789462703537
ebook

Islamophobia as a Form of
Radicalisation Perspectives
on Media, Academia and
Socio-political Scapes from
Europe and Canada

Leen d'Haenens, Abdelwahed
Mekki-Berrada (eds)

€ 25,00 / £25.00 | PB
ISBN 9789462703698
Open Access ebook

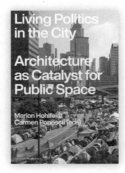

Living Politics in the City Architecture as
Catalyst for Public Space
Marion Hohlfeldt, Carmen Popescu (eds)

€ 59,50 / £53.00 | PB
ISBN 9789462703599

HOW TO ORDER

Sales representation and Order fulfilment UK: Ingram Publisher Services UK – distribution.nbni.co.uk - IPSUK.Cservs@ingramcontent.com
Sales representation USA: Cornell University Press - www.cornellpress.cornell.edu -
Order fulfilment USA: Longleaf Services, Inc. - customerservice@longleafservices.org

ORDER ONLINE AT WWW.LUP.BE